FREYA STARK IN IRAQ AND KUWAIT

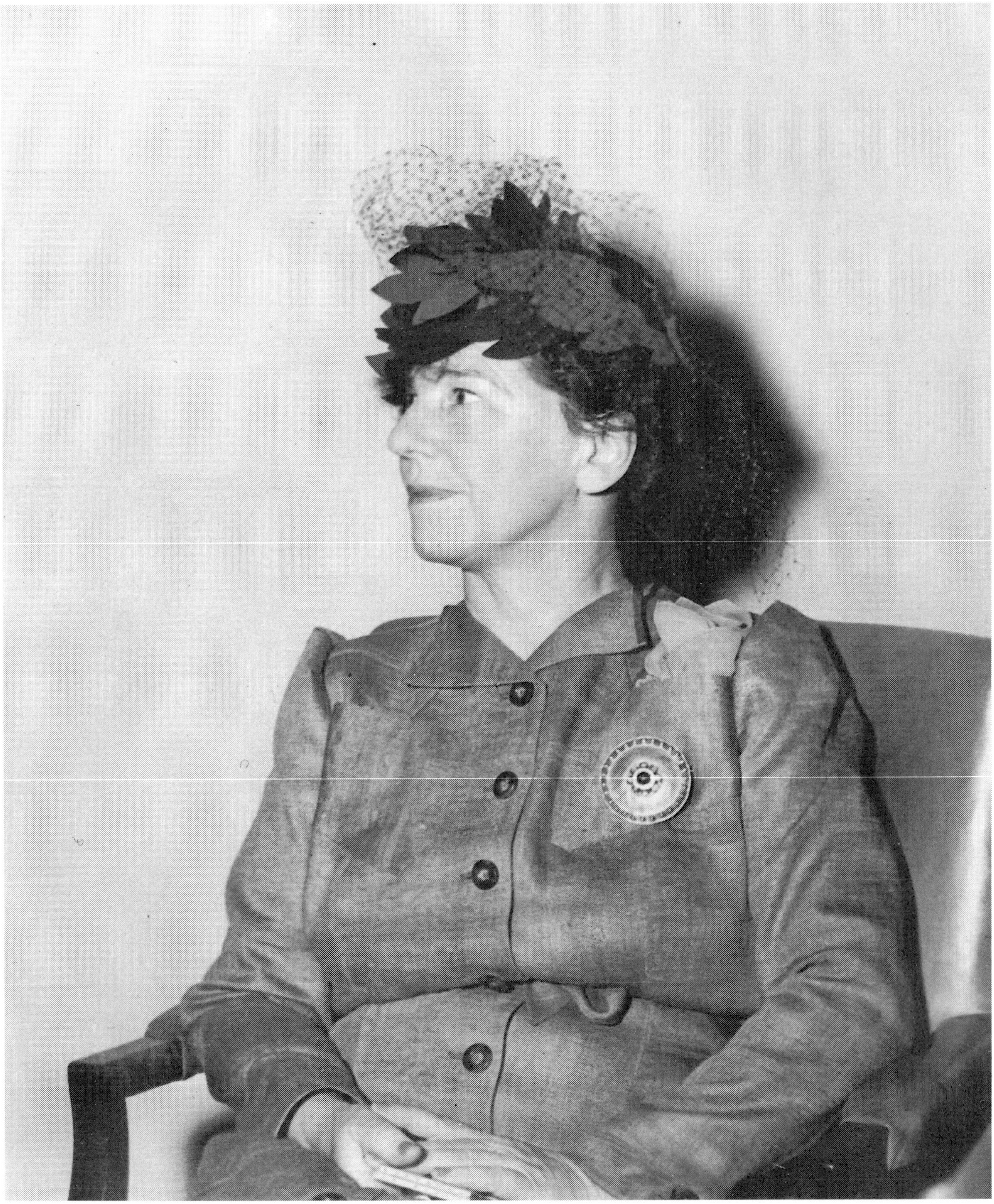

Freya Stark

MALISE RUTHVEN

FREYA STARK

IN IRAQ AND KUWAIT

GARNET PUBLISHING

First Edition

ISBN: 1 85964 004 4

British Library Cataloguing-in-Publication Data.
A catalogue record for this book is available from the British Library.

The photograph of Freya Stark on page 2 is reproduced courtesy of John Murray (Publishers) Ltd, with grateful thanks.

Design by Elizabeth van Amerongen
Cover design by Arthur op den Brouw
House editor Anna Watson
Typeset by Columns Ltd, Reading
Reproduction by CCTS, London
Printed in the Lebanon

Published by Garnet Publishing Ltd,
8 Southern Court, South Street,
Reading RG1 4QS, UK.

CONTENTS

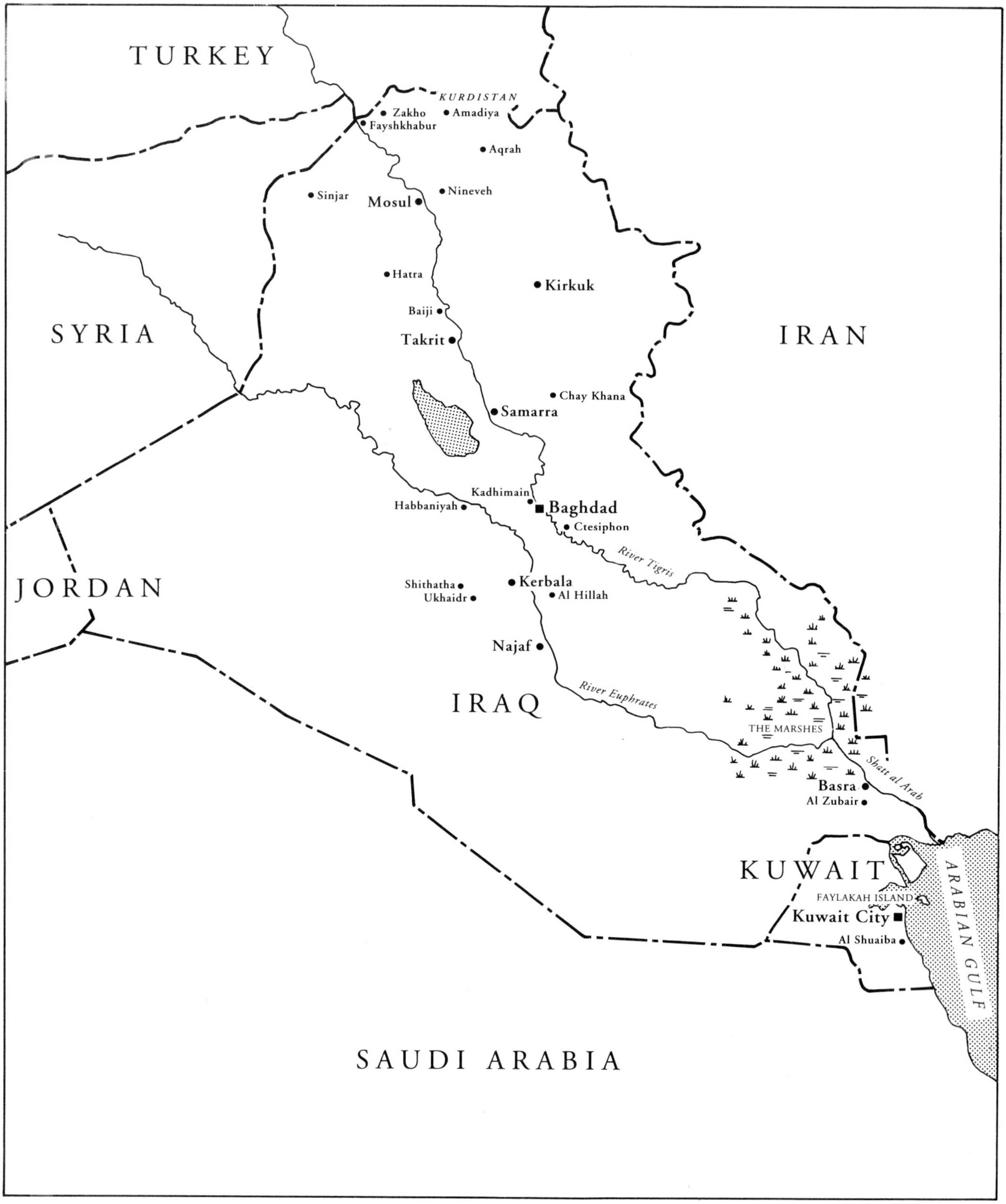
TURKEY
KURDISTAN
Zakho
Amadiya
Fayshkhabur
Aqrah
Sinjar
Mosul
Nineveh
Hatra
Kirkuk
Baiji
SYRIA
Takrit
IRAN
Chay Khana
Samarra
Kadhimain
Habbaniyah
Baghdad
Ctesiphon
River Tigris
JORDAN
Shithatha
Kerbala
Ukhaidr
Al Hillah
Najaf
IRAQ
River Euphrates
THE MARSHES
Shatt al Arab
Basra
Al Zubair
KUWAIT
FAYLAKAH ISLAND
Kuwait City
Al Shuaiba
ARABIAN GULF
SAUDI ARABIA

INTRODUCTION

Freya Stark made her first expedition to Iraq in March 1929, travelling by car from Damascus. The excitement of the journey was captured in an article she wrote for the English-language *Baghdad Times*, published in 1937 as *Baghdad Sketches*. "In the open desert", she wrote, "there is romance even in the motor. There is no high road except such as is made by the track of previous wheels and is blotted out by every rain. Far and near, before you and behind, cars of every kind speed over the uninhabited earth. They roll its sands in spirals like a pillar of cloud behind them, or shine with headlights, like a column of fire by night." At the last French frontier-post she had the opportunity to inspect the motley collection of vehicles: rickety vans bound for Mecca, packed with white-robed pilgrims and piled to the ceiling with packages; the long grey chassis of the Nairn overland buses; the crowd of small cars – Chevrolets, Morrises, Fiats and Fords "in every stage of smartness and dilapidation, but chiefly the latter, with every variety of box and bundle bulging at back and sides".

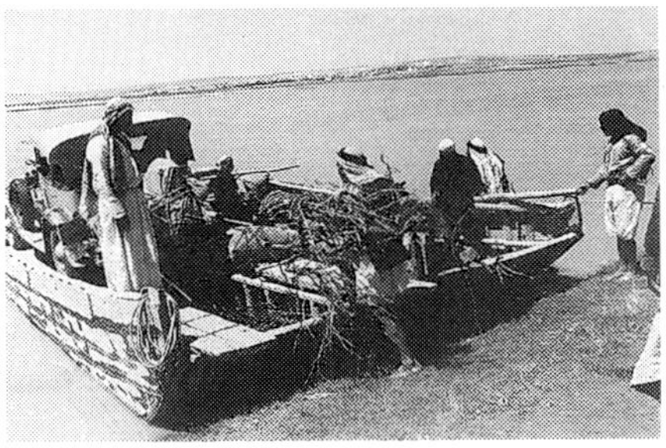

Crossing the Euphrates

Baghdad, the city of the Caliphs, was undergoing a gradual but inexorable transformation. After centuries of provincial stagnation under the Ottomans, the city of the Arabian Nights was a capital once more, though no longer the seat of an empire. Created out of the three former Ottoman provinces of Basra, Baghdad and Mosul, the state of Iraq was mandated to the British by the Treaty of San Remo in April 1920. The British had supplied the country with an Arab king, Feisal, son of the Sharif of Mecca and leader, with help from T. E. Lawrence, of the Arab revolt against the Turks during the First World War. There was a bicameral legislature and what was supposed to be a democratic system of government. Every Iraqi minister, however, had at his shoulder a British adviser whose advice had to be taken. Ultimate authority lay in the hands of the British High Commissioner and the commander of the Royal Air Force. Iraqi political power, such as it was, was controlled by a small urban clique in uneasy alliance with powerful tribal leaders. In the words of a visiting British cabinet minister in 1925: "If the writ of King Feisal runs effectively throughout his kingdom it is entirely due to British aeroplanes. If the aeroplanes were removed tomorrow, the whole structure would inevitably fall to pieces."

Although the mandate formally ended in 1932, real power remained with the British Embassy and the clique of politicians, led by Nuri al-Said, the former Ottoman army officer who had fought with Feisal and Lawrence, who continued to manipulate the system to their advantage. The Iraqi oil fields surrounding the northern town of Kirkuk had been awarded to the Iraq Petroleum Company, an Anglo-French–American consortium in 1925. As war with Germany approached the British Government considered it essential that access to the oilfields should be controlled by the British.

Under British tutelage Baghdad was expanding. A pontoon bridge spanned the Tigris and a modern high street of asphalt, lined with new shops, sprang up next to the traditional Arab town. As well as advisors the British supplied the monarchy with plumed hats, open landaus, modern communications and a large staff of bureaucrats, engineers and teachers. The majority of Baghdad's inhabitants, a heterogeneous mix of ethnic and religious affiliates, including Arab Sunnis and Shiites, Kurds, Armenian and Chaldean Christians, Jews, Lurs, Assyrians and Bedouin from the desert, went about their business as before, each marked by distinctive manner of speech, appearance and dress. There were also ominous signs of the future challenge to British power and influence in the emergence of a nationalist bourgeoisie whose desire for leadership had been frustrated by the British presence.

Freya was fascinated by the juxtaposition of ancient and modern to be found in the East, where a medieval society had been overlaid with the products and processes of the industrial revolution without the much longer period of adjustment and adaptation that occurred in the West. Slavery still existed among the Bedouin and in Kuwait, where one could purchase a black baby for 20 rupees. Her housemaid, Marie, a "dark, untidy loquacious creature", like the beautiful wife of Sheikh Habib whom she met in the desert, was an Armenian who had been captured into slavery and married to a Bedouin after the massacres of her people by the Turks. Being a good ethnographer, Freya preferred to observe than to moralise. "How lucky one is . . . to combine in a single lifetime such an astonishing variety of friends and surroundings. Here one can see history as she is, the mosaic of times and places, fantastic strands visibly interweaving, ruled only by the compulsion of land and water and dust."

At first, Freya's decision to live among the people of Baghdad in the "native" quarter was a source of scandal. Brought up in Italy and in England among artists, she was shocked at the petty snobbery and racism of the class of administrators and officials who ran the Mandatory regime. She regarded the English women as more culpable than their husbands. "A dreadful conclusion is forced on one as one travels. The British appear to be popular wherever they go until they come to settle with their wives. The mere fact that such an importation makes the home more pleasant than it was causes an exclusion, though an unavoidable one, of the outer world. It creates a barrier which was not there before they came."

An experience that sharpened her awareness of the "memsahib factor" in colonial administration was her acceptance of an invitation to stay with two women friends as guests of Sheikh Habib, a cousin of her Arabic teacher. Her original companions succumbed to pressure from their husbands to abandon the trip, and she was put under strong pressure to do likewise. Eventually she found another companion in Mrs Drower, the wife of the legal adviser to the Iraqi Government, who spoke fluent Arabic. The episode, which reminded her of E. M. Forster's *Passage to India*, brought her round to accepting with some reluctance the necessity for Iraqi independence.

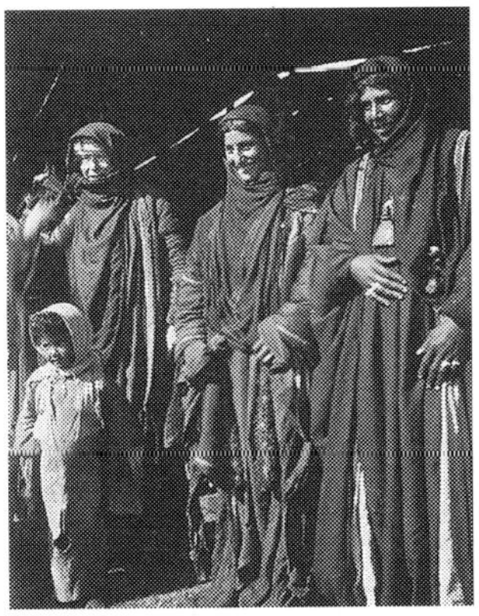

Bedouin women
1930

At heart she would remain an imperialist. She believed in the paternalistic assumptions inherent in the Mandate, "one of the most revolutionary measures ever invented by an Imperial power", which, in accordance with Article 22 of the Covenant of the League of Nations, provided for the government of "peoples not yet able to stand by themselves under the strenuous conditions of the modern world." She believed strongly in the disinterested character of British justice and administration, and she was highly critical of the French, whose roughshod interpretation of the Mandate in Syria she regarded as the height of political cynicism. Her vision of Empire was essentially romantic. She idealized the British colonial administrators who understood the East and spoke its languages – men like Vyvian Holt, who had succeeded Gertrude Bell as Oriental Secretary, Sir Kinahan Cornwallis, the High Commissioner and Gerald de Gaury, who worked in intelligence and later became Resident in Kuwait. Like Kipling she believed in the benevolent mixing of peoples and races under the rule of an enlightened British élite. By blaming the wives for the snobbery and racism she saw around her, she was able to maintain the vision while deploring much of the reality.

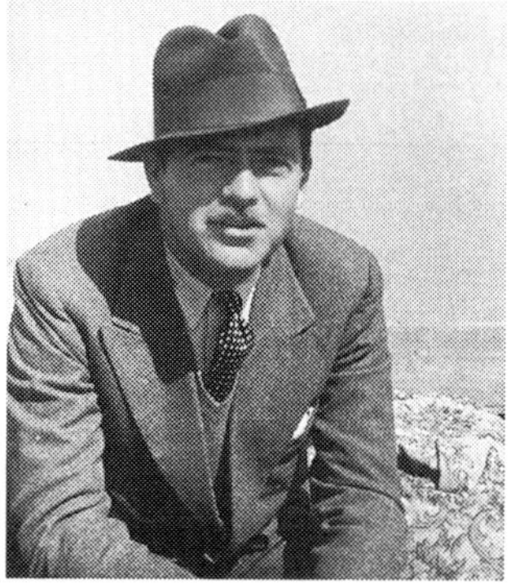

Gerald de Gaury
1937

Like many Europeans before her, Freya also tended to idealize the "free" peoples of the country such as Bedouin Arabs and Kurds, at the expense of the bourgeois townees who were beginning to adopt European manners and dress. She discerned a "natural affinity" between the desert Arabs and the English. "The love of personal independence, the equal human status under God, have a peculiar likeness to those things which an Englishman in his heart is most ready to fight for." Sheikh 'Ajil of the Shammar, whom she met in March 1930 she compared, nostalgically, to the English country squires she knew from her childhood in Devon. Like his English counterpart, the sheikh was "becoming an anachronism: the Latin centralizing conception is ousting the old personal ideas which were common to our Teutonic forefathers and to the Beduin of the desert . . . the differences between the feudalism of the East and that of our public schools and universities was not so great as one might think: and there were many points of contact between a tribal chieftain and the sons of English country gentlemen who ran the Empire."

In contrast to these supposedly authentic representatives of the Orient, she initially shared the general British disdain for the "young effendis", as she called the newly emerging class of western-educated bourgeois youth who would challenge British power. "To be anti-British made you successful either as a lawyer, a politician or a journalist; you made an income, and you were a patriot as well, which is as near as one can get in politics to eating one's cake and having it." She held the administration's educational policies responsible for the virus of nationalism: "With our usual disinterestedness . . . we spare no effort in producing as many of them as we can; we make them out of the sons of desert sheikhs, of Jewish merchants, of landholders and officials – all people who might be friendly until we so educate them as to produce an Energy for which at present there is no sufficient outlet and which can find its only way of existence in political agitations."

Freya was an artist, however, more than an intellectual, and analytical consistency was never one of her virtues. She may have romanticized the tribesfolk under the mistaken impression that they were freer from social constraints than urbanites. But she was too sharp an observer of reality, and had too much empathy with people at a human level, to deny the "young effendis" their aspirations. In a perceptive essay "The young Effendi and the sentimental traveller" included in *Baghdad Sketches,* she addressed some of the themes that would surface in the debate over representations, or misrepresentations, of the orient launched by the critic Edward Said half a century later. The sentimental traveller, as she preferred to call the vulgar orientalist, had had his innings. "He travelled when picturesque antiquity still held the reins of Asia and, seeing the young ideas as they began their first feeble struggles here and there, uncritically and unkindly stamped upon them." The modernists, represented by the "young effendis", had found it difficult to get their message across, not least because of the facile appeal orientalism held for the Western imagination. "It is a fact that people can visualize the charms of a tribal chief in native dress more easily than those of, say, a bank clerk in coat and tie . . ." The young effendi often reacted with shrillness and arrogance: but the inferiority complex he thus revealed was misplaced. He failed to address the flaw in the sentimental traveller's position. The latter made an unfair comparison between the old and the new according to their momentary value, instead of measuring past achievement against future potential. Despite recognizing the value of the old ways, Freya was not a sentimentalist. She welcomed progress, and came to recognise that its direction would inevitably lie in nationalist hands. On returning to Iraq during the Second World War, she engaged the "young effendis" directly, with a view to luring them away from the totalitarian mirage to which, in their hostility to the British, they were inevitably drawn. Her conversion, however, came much too late to make any difference. By the end of the war the Hashemite monarchy, discredited by its association with Britain, was unable to function as the symbol around which the national Iraqi identity would rally.

The slump in Europe and North America had severely reduced Freya's modest private income, and it was in Baghdad in 1932 that, for the first and only time in her life, she became a professional journalist, as a sub-editor on the English-language *Baghdad Times*. Her main task was to put the news, culled from the BBC, the *Daily Mail* and Reuters telegrams 'into English'. She quarrelled with sloppy adjectives and occasionally teased her editor, Mr

Cameron, with facetious headlines. A story about a professor who died in front of his class after mistaking a beaker full of acid for a glass of water was given the headline "An Absent-Minded End". This particular headline did not get past Mr Cameron's desk, though he was sufficiently impressed by her skills to offer her "a job at any time".

Freya made several expeditions from her base in Baghdad during the early 1930s. Apart from the award-winning journeys to the Elburz Mountains and Luristan (see *Freya Stark in Persia*) she visited Mosul, Takrit, the Shammar tribes and the Yezidi "Devil Worshippers" in the north. Under the protection of the veil she visited the holy Shiite shrines of Kadhimain, near Baghdad, and Najaf, normally forbidden to Christians. She made two visits to Kuwait, in 1932 and 1937. As yet the shadow of the oil boom was "no bigger than a man's hand". She returned to Baghdad in April 1941, having served in Aden and Cairo as a propagandist for the Ministry of Information. As part of her campaign to rally support for the British war effort in Iraq she made a ten-day tour of Kurdistan in 1942 and visited the marshes north of Basra, in 1943.

The circumstances of her return to Baghdad in wartime were highly dramatic. On leave from Cairo, she had decided to spend some time in Persia, but cut short her holiday after the pro-German coup launched by four Iraqi generals, popularly known as the "Golden Square", who took control of the army and surrounded the Regent's palace with troops. At the time the king, Feisal II, was only seven years old and his uncle Abdul-Ilah, was in charge. The latter escaped from the palace, hiding beneath the cushions in the American Minister's car. The colonels deposed him, appointing a Regent of their own. Parliament was summoned and endorsed a new government under the veteran nationalist politician Rashid Ali al-Gailani which was more sympathetic to the Germans.

The British were in a delicate position. Under the terms of the 1930 Treaty of Alliance, Iraq was obliged to make its railways, rivers and ports available to Britain, as well as the RAF base at Habbaniyah (used mainly as a training establishment). To avoid giving the British any excuse for moving against him, Rashid Ali declared that he intended strictly to observe the terms of the treaty. Churchill, however, decided that the situation was too dangerous to leave to diplomacy at a critical time during the war and resolved to use force. A brigade, diverted from Burma, was landed at Basra, and the incoming ambassador, Sir Kinahan Cornwallis, intimated that British recognition of the new government would only be forthcoming if the troops were allowed to land. Rashid Ali agreed to this, but baulked at a second landing of troops before the first had left. The situation became extremely tense, with increasingly vociferous nationalist demonstrators taking to the streets. Soon the British Embassy was under siege. The British reinforced the base at Habbaniyah. Women and children were evacuated by air to Basra. The Iraqis moved a brigade to the plateau overlooking the air base, and issued orders forbidding the Iraqis to fly. The commander of the base (Air Vice-Marshal Smart) with Churchill's backing, decided to attack the Iraqis from the air before they had time to shell the base. The RAF used everything it had – elderly Wellingtons, uncamouflaged Audaxes, ageing Oxfords and a motley collection of training aircraft flown, in the absence of proper pilots, by uncertified pupils. After five days of intense bombing and counter-shelling, the Iraqis collapsed, their brigade at al-Fallujah destroyed. Other army commanders wavered.

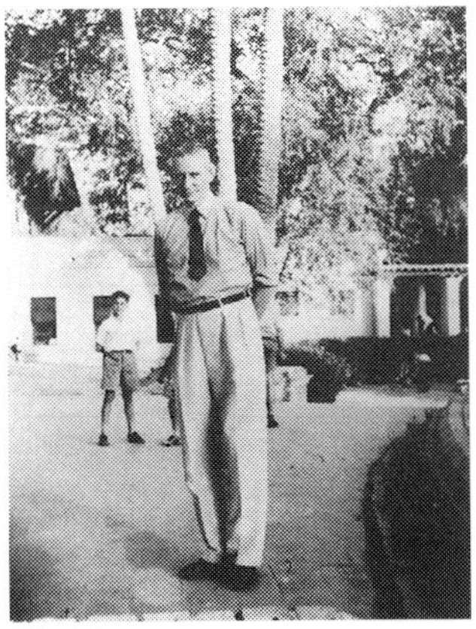

Sir K. Cornwallis in the besieged Baghdad Embassy May 1941

Freya managed to get back from Persia just before the Embassy gates were finally closed. The siege lasted more than three weeks while the battle for Iraq raged round the Habbaniyah base. About 350 people had taken refuge in the Embassy compound, including Indians, Iraqi Jews, British Embassy staff and Iraqi servants. Freya shared a dormitory with sixteen women in Lady Cornwallis's magnificent bedroom overlooking the river. In the ballroom downstairs, the refugees huddled in groups, surrounded by their belongings. Freya noticed how much better adapted the Easterners were to this style of life than the Europeans. With carpets and samovars usually at hand, they would instinctively form a circle "while we, each defending his own privacy, vainly try to make small barricades of our boxes and belongings". Food was scarce, but available. After a week, during which all the stores were consumed, Captain Holt, the Oriental Secretary, arranged through his contacts in the Iraqi Foreign Ministry to buy supplies. There were still people in government who sympathized with the British – or at least were prepared to put some money on a British victory, and they were proved right. A Jordanian–British force arrived across the desert and by the end of May the siege was lifted and Freya went back to Cairo.

She returned to Baghdad the following year, to establish an Iraqi branch of the Brotherhood of Freedom, the anti-Axis, pro-democracy organization she had successfully launched in Egypt. The movement was never as successful in Iraq as it was in Egypt, where the spirit of democracy was stronger and the prospect of a German victory less congenial to a population aware of the real experience of Italian colonialism in neighbouring Libya. At the Brotherhood's headquarters at South Gate, young Iraqi intellectuals were welcomed to discuss the issues of the day in an atmosphere that was intended to be free from crude propaganda. But the Iraqi army, seething from its humiliating defeat by the British, remained largely pro-German at heart. German advances in Russia, the entry of Japan in the war in December 1941, the fall of Singapore in February 1942 and of Tobruk the following June persuaded many that a successful German push to the Gulf was only a matter of time. A handful of officers – about 30 – joined Freya's committees, as did some of the Iraqi generals' wives. But it was the Allied victory of Alamein (October 1942) followed by the German defeat at Stalingrad (February 1943) rather than the Brotherhood's propaganda, that impressed the Iraqis. Their resentment against the British smouldered on long after the war and erupted, like a dormant volcano, in 1958 when General Abdul Karim al-Qasim overthrew the monarchy in a violent and bloody coup d'état. The Arab statesman whom Freya most admired, the Prime Minister, Nuri al Said, was shot while trying to escape in women's clothes. Freya never forgave the young officers and the "effendis" who supported them. She never returned to Iraq after the revolution, and for the rest of her life would refer to the revolutionaries as "murderers".

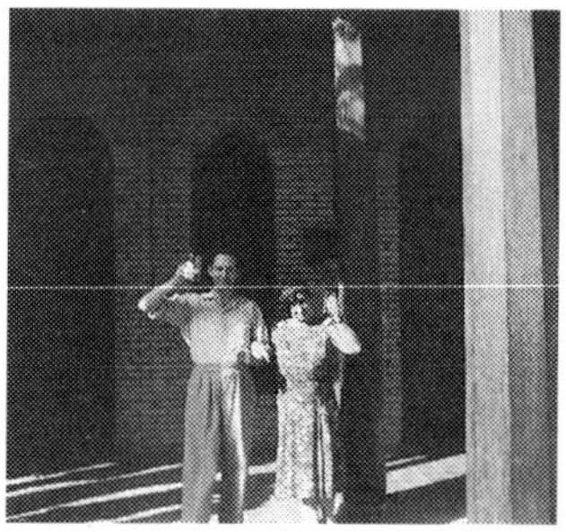

Relief of the Embassy

IRAQ

NORTHERN IRAQ

Freya Stark made several visits to northern Iraq before, during and after the Second World War. In March 1930 she travelled to Mosul with Mrs Drower, the Arabic-speaking wife of the legal adviser to the Iraqi Government, who had taken Freya under her wing. They went by train to Baiji and then drove for six hours by car over a carpet of desert grass coloured with wild tulips, anemones, mignonette and marigolds. The bazaars of Mosul were filled with colourful costumes: Kurds with baggy trousers and padded waistcoats, Tiaris with soft felt hats and "shrewd mountaineers faces", Christians wearing bright colours and baggier trousers than the Kurds.

After exploring the ancient site of Nineveh the two women went into the desert as guest of Sheikh 'Ajil of the Shammar. They had a large tent to themselves, furnished with white mattresses and purple cushions. They were surrounded by the sheikh's family and slaves, with horses, donkeys, camels, foals and children grazing or playing outside, enjoying the short delicious spring. "One has a wonderful feeling of safety and protection within the limits of the tribe," wrote Freya in one of her letters. "The fierce thick furry dogs roam about the outskirts ready to attack wolves or strangers."

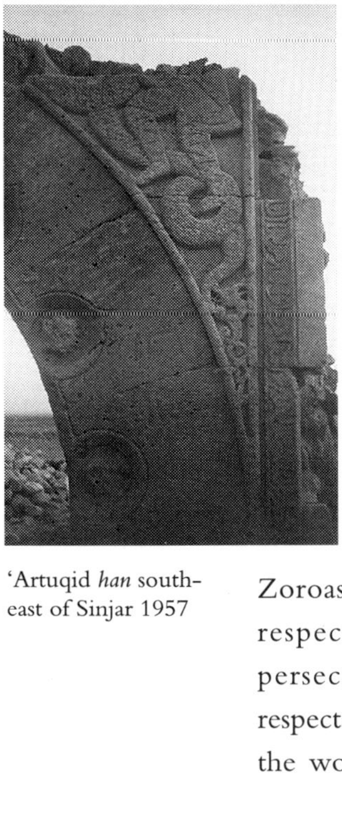

'Artuqid *han* south-east of Sinjar 1957

In Sheikh 'Ajil's tent, where the slaves served them with huge trays of rice and meat on a tablecloth of red and orange gazelle skins, they met a sheikh of the mysterious Yezidi sect, known as devil-worshippers, who had arrived from Sinjar, west of Mosul, with his attendants. The two women went on to visit the shrine of the Yezidis at Sheikh 'Adi, in an enchanted mountain valley of figs and oaks and flowering shrubs, filled with the sounds of birds and running water. The survivors of pre-Islamic, gnostic and Zoroastrian cults, the Yezidis were a peaceful, agricultural people. The respect they paid to the Devil was often misunderstood and led to persecution by their Muslim neighbours. Believing like many more respectable people that the Prince of Darkness had been given a free hand in the world, they went out of their way to avoid giving him offence. They avoided blue, the colour of heaven, and all words beginning with the *sh* of Shaytan, and abstained from lettuces or radishes, two plants which refused to hide Satan beneath their leaves after his expulsion from heaven. The wall of their temple, once a Chaldean church, was adorned with Satan's symbol – a black snake carved in relief, similar to those found on ancient Luristan daggers or prehistoric Persian earthenware.

On a subsequent visit to the north with Mrs Drower and her daughter Peggy in 1937 Freya stopped at Takrit, birthplace of Saladin and, notoriously, the home town of Saddam Hussein and his fellow Takritis now ruling Iraq through the Ba'ath party. They visited Samarra, the ancient Abbasid capital, "a lovely sight like a Persian miniature" with its ancient spiral tower and golden dome and minarets.

In 1942 Freya was sent by the Embassy to tour Kurdistan and was pleased to find that the tribesmen were staunchly pro-British. "They all come up in their turbans and big woollen suits slung about with guns and cartridges and say: 'we are ready to fight for you whenever you want us'," she wrote. One of the villages she visited was Hallabja, where several hundred Kurds were murdered by the Iraqi army in a poison gas attack in March 1988.

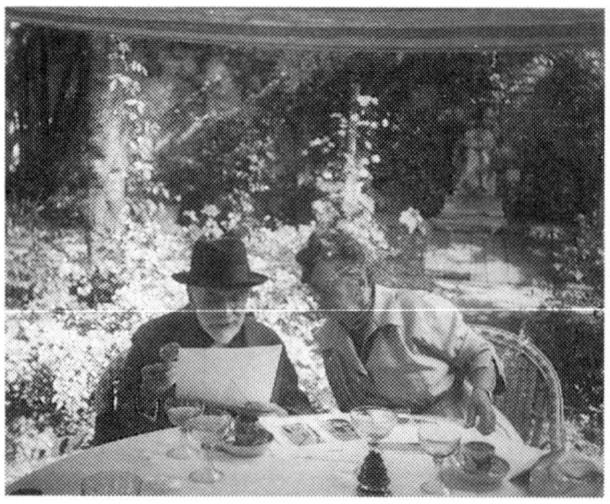

Freya Stark with Bernard Berenson in the garden at Asolo 1955

In 1957, on her last visit to Iraq, Freya returned to Sheikh 'Adi to attend a Yezidi feast and watched a little black heifer being sacrificed among the crowd of young men and gaily decked-out women. "It was the most pagan thing I have seen short of the Southern Indian temples," she told her friend the art historian Bernard Berenson. "Nowhere else here does one see the women, unveiled and gorgeous, mix freely with the men. A great depth is given to a scene when every trifle, and every costume, has a meaning: the tradition is a living stream on which all the separate lives are floating."

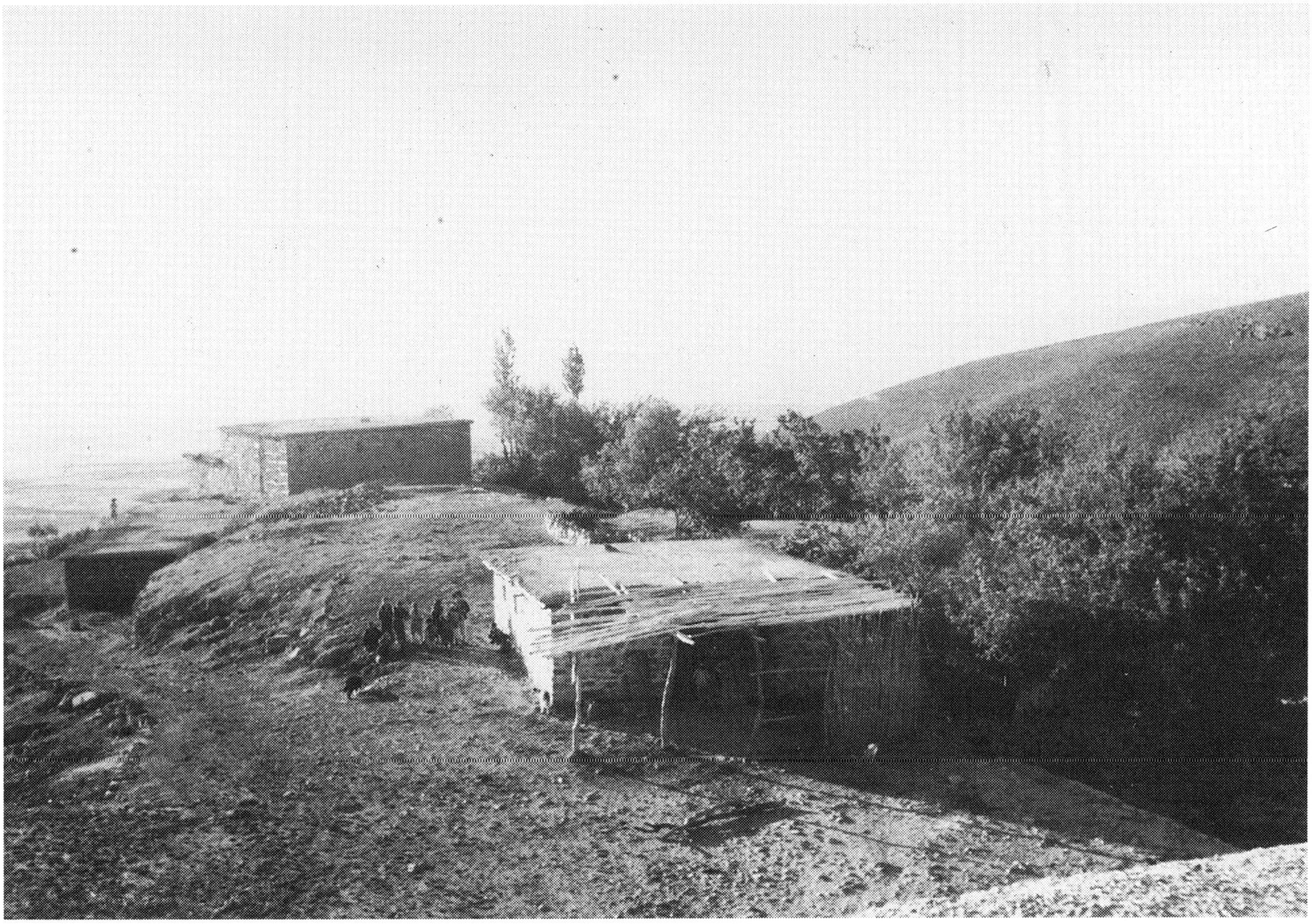

Hallabja, Kurdistan 1942

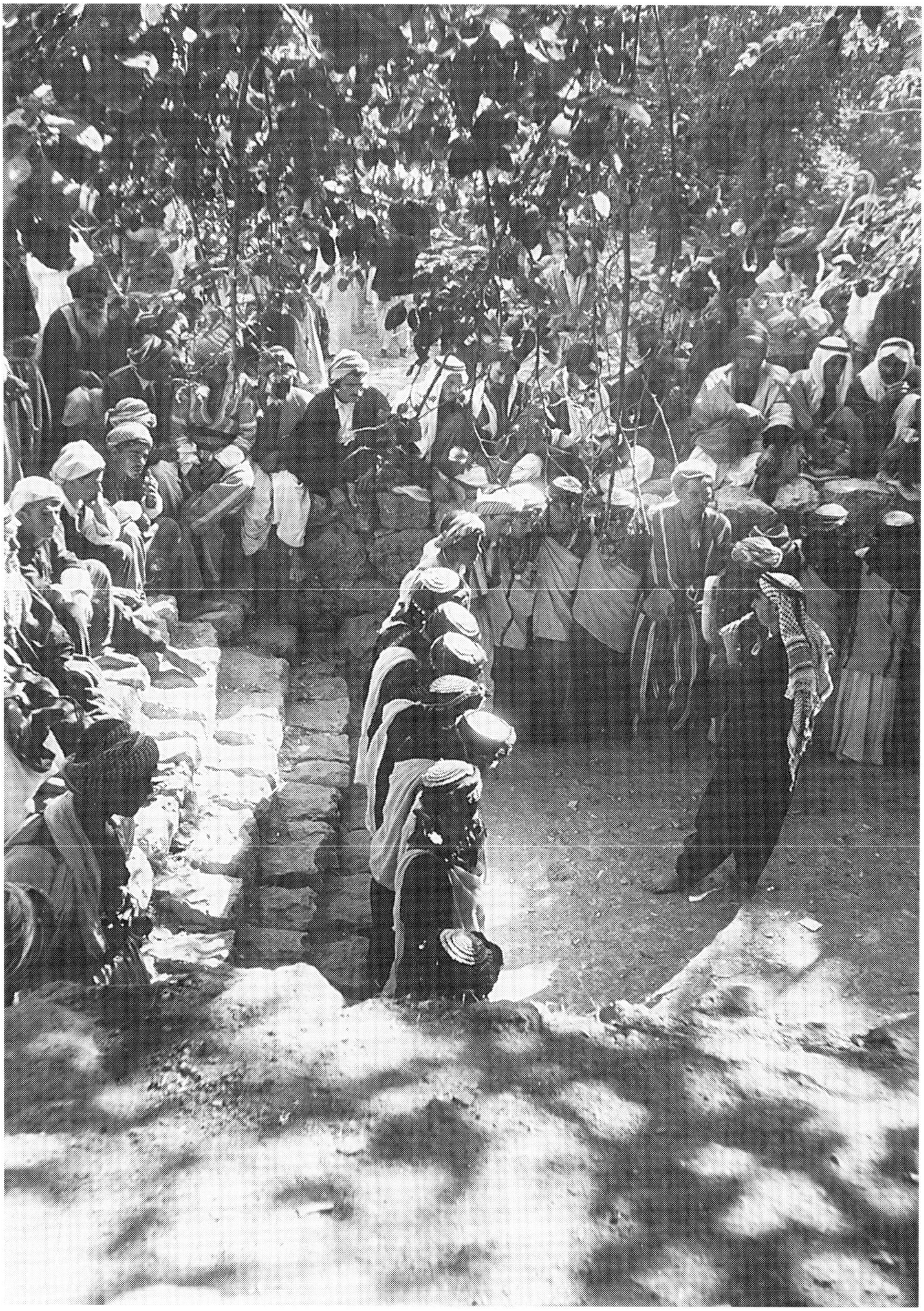

Yezidis at Sheikh 'Adi, 1957

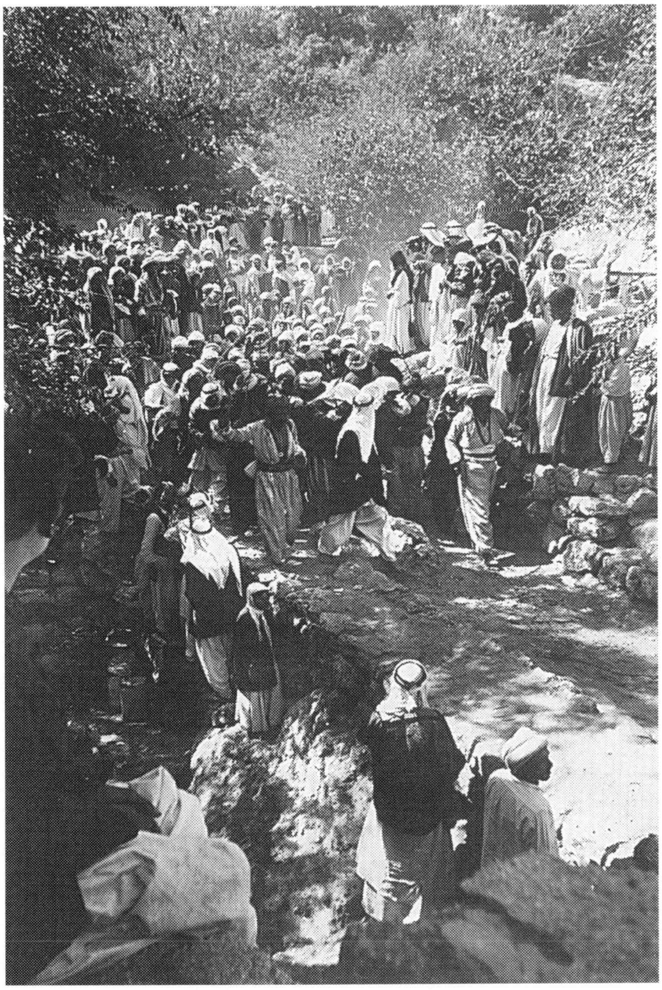

Yezidis at Sheikh 'Adi, 1957

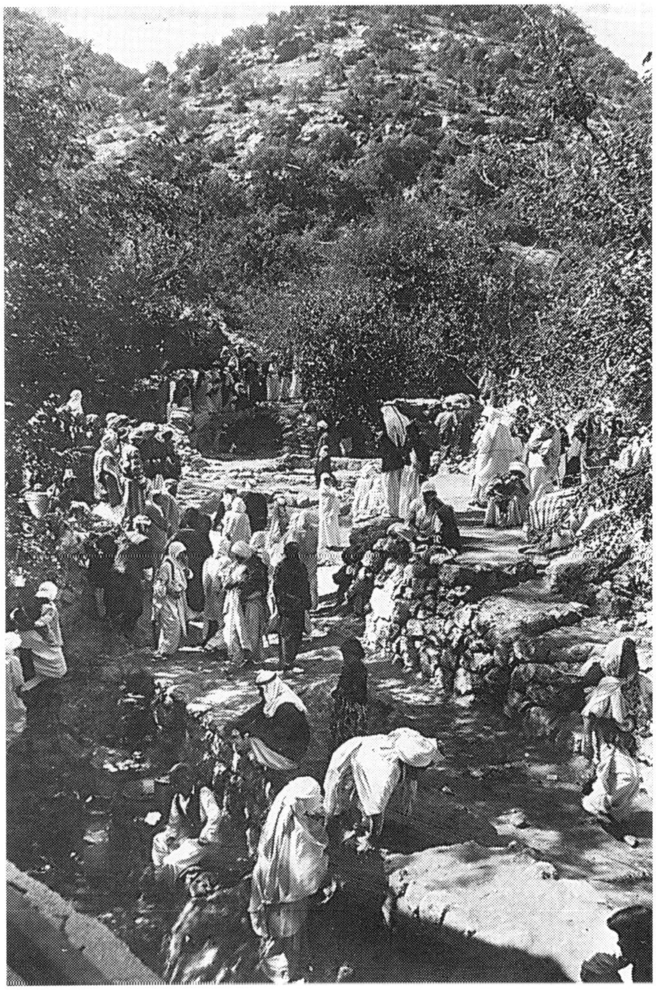

Yezidis at Sheikh 'Adi, 1957

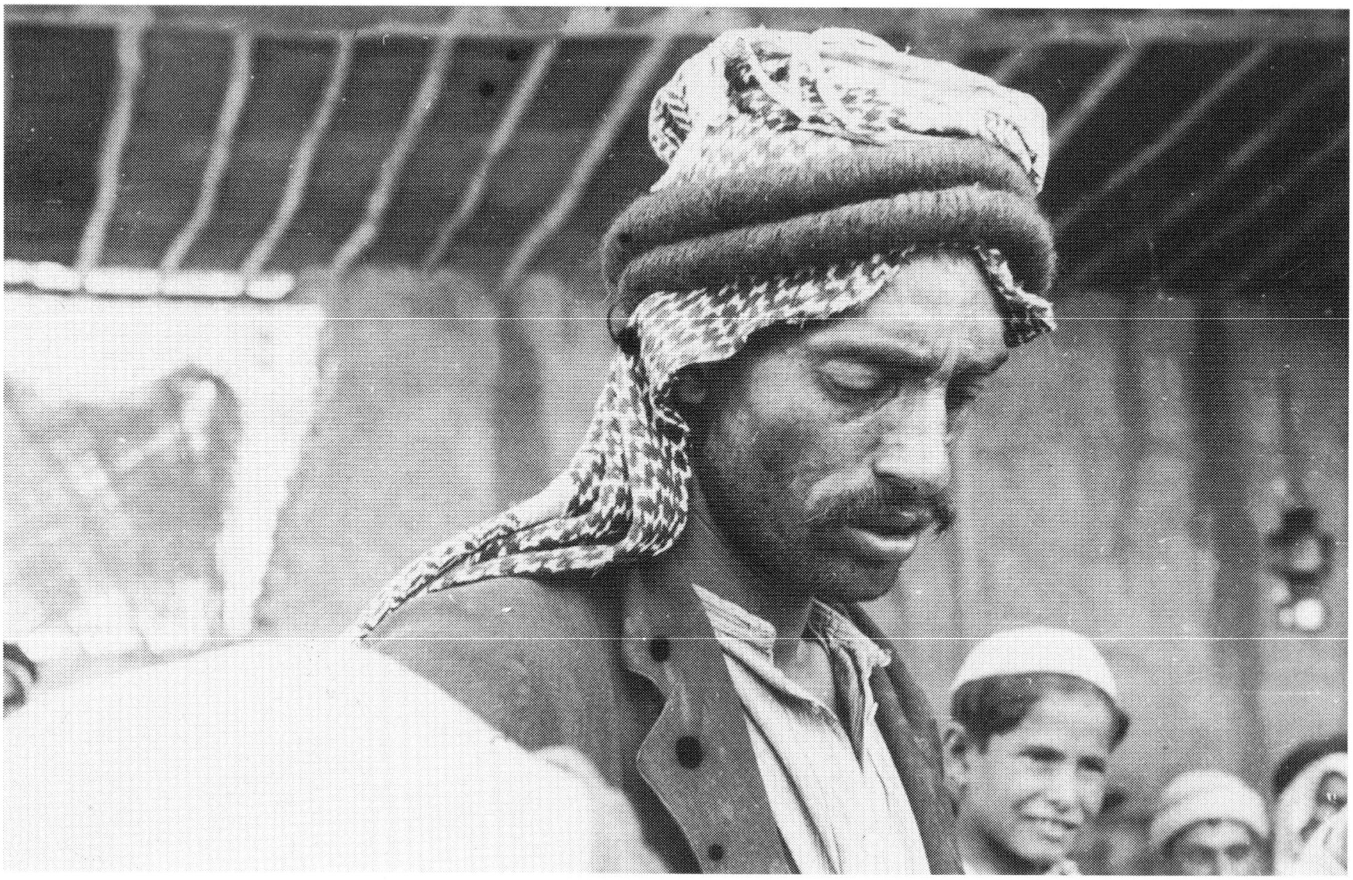

Takrit 1937

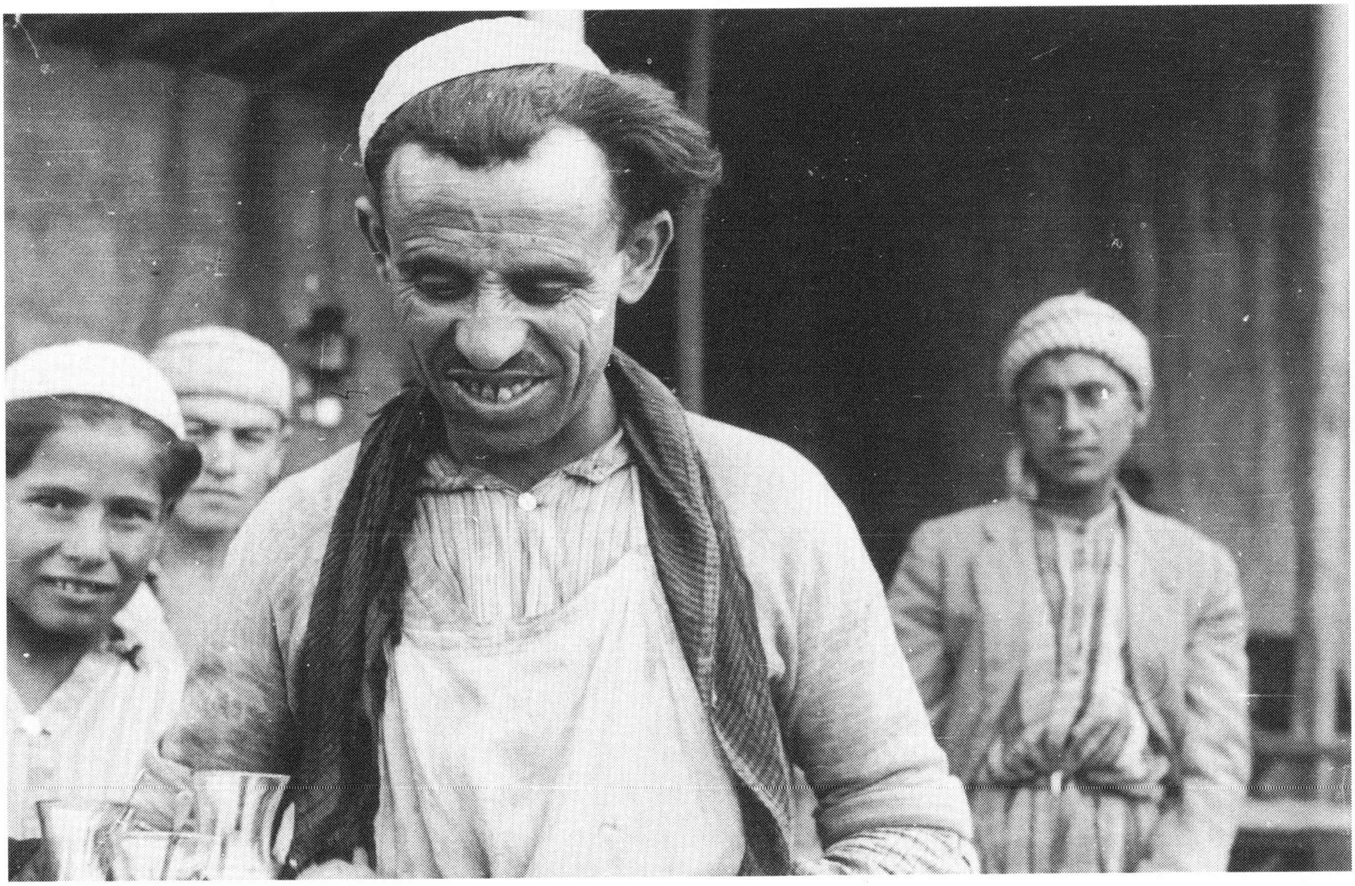

Takrit coffee shop 1930

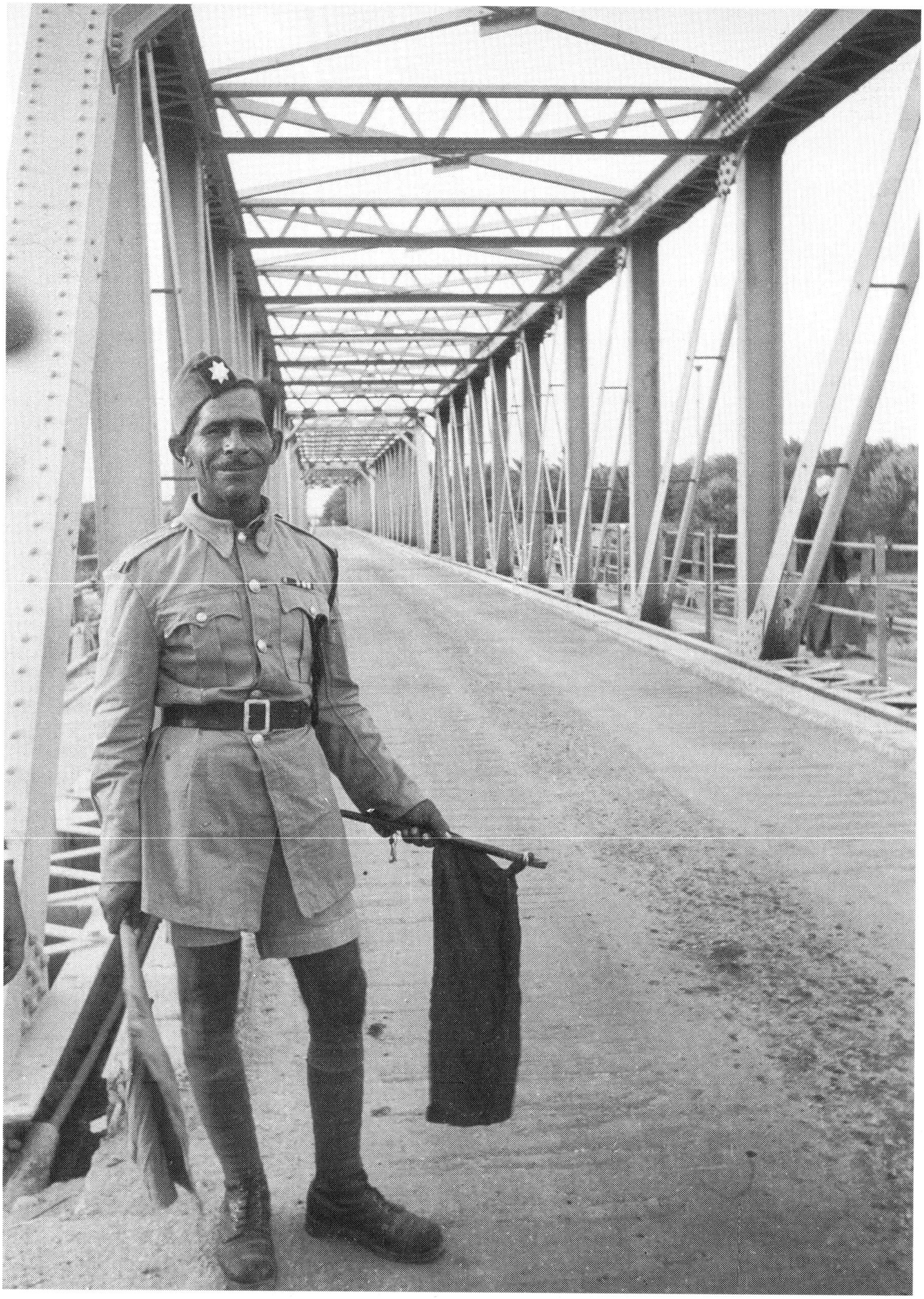

Bridge over the Diyala river 1957

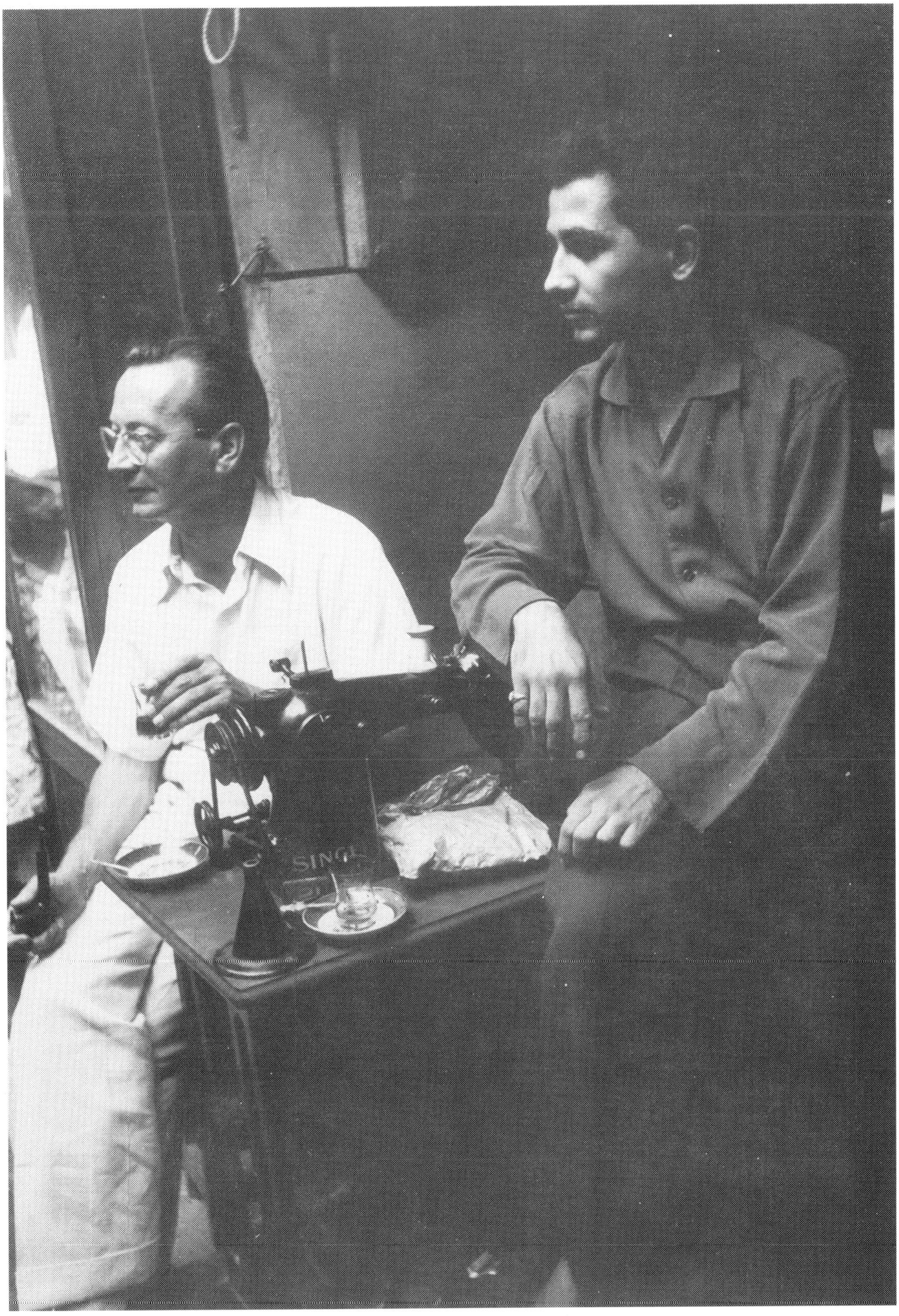

Wilfred Kirkpatrick and Arab friend, Kirkuk 1957

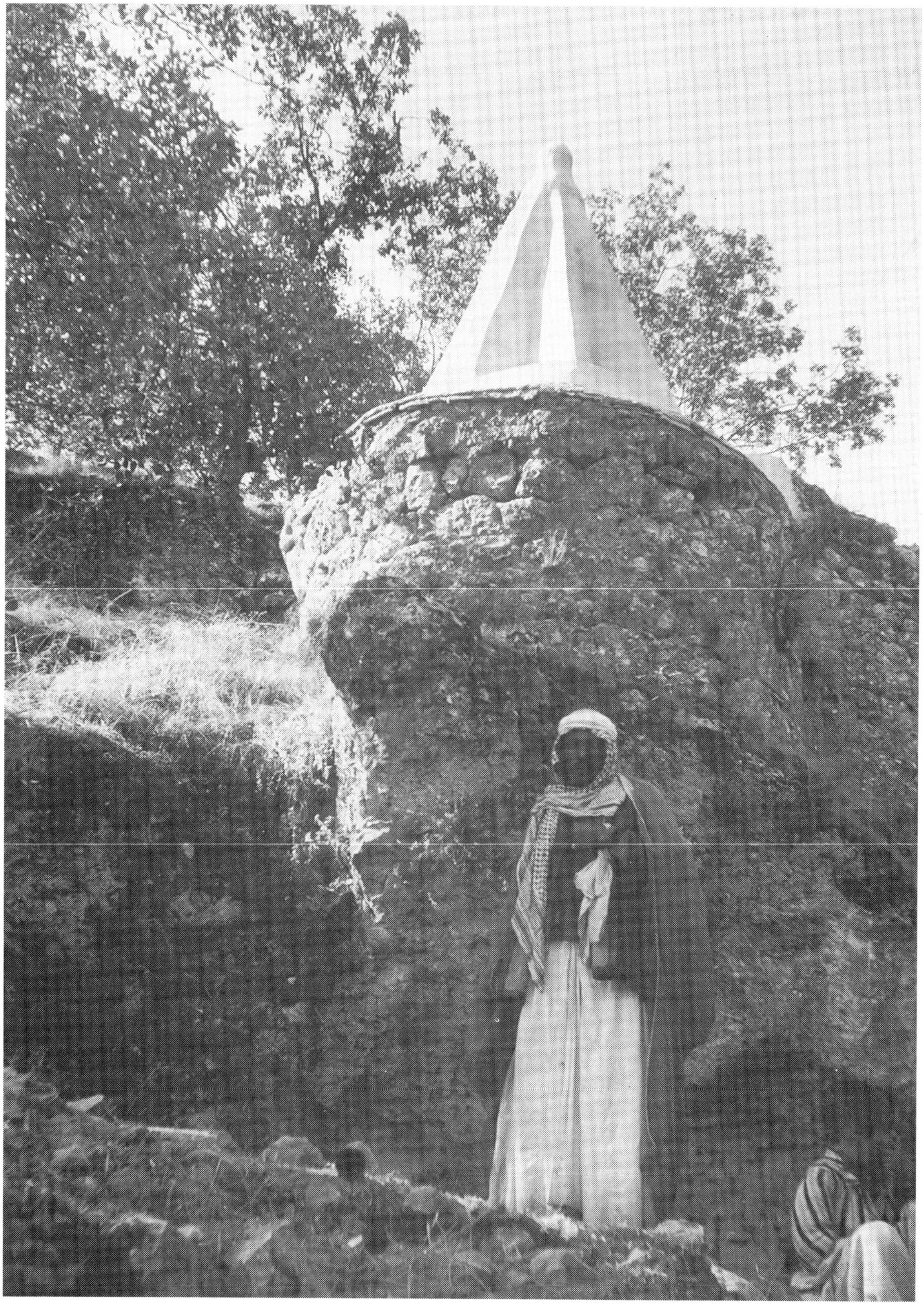

Sheikh 'Adi 1957

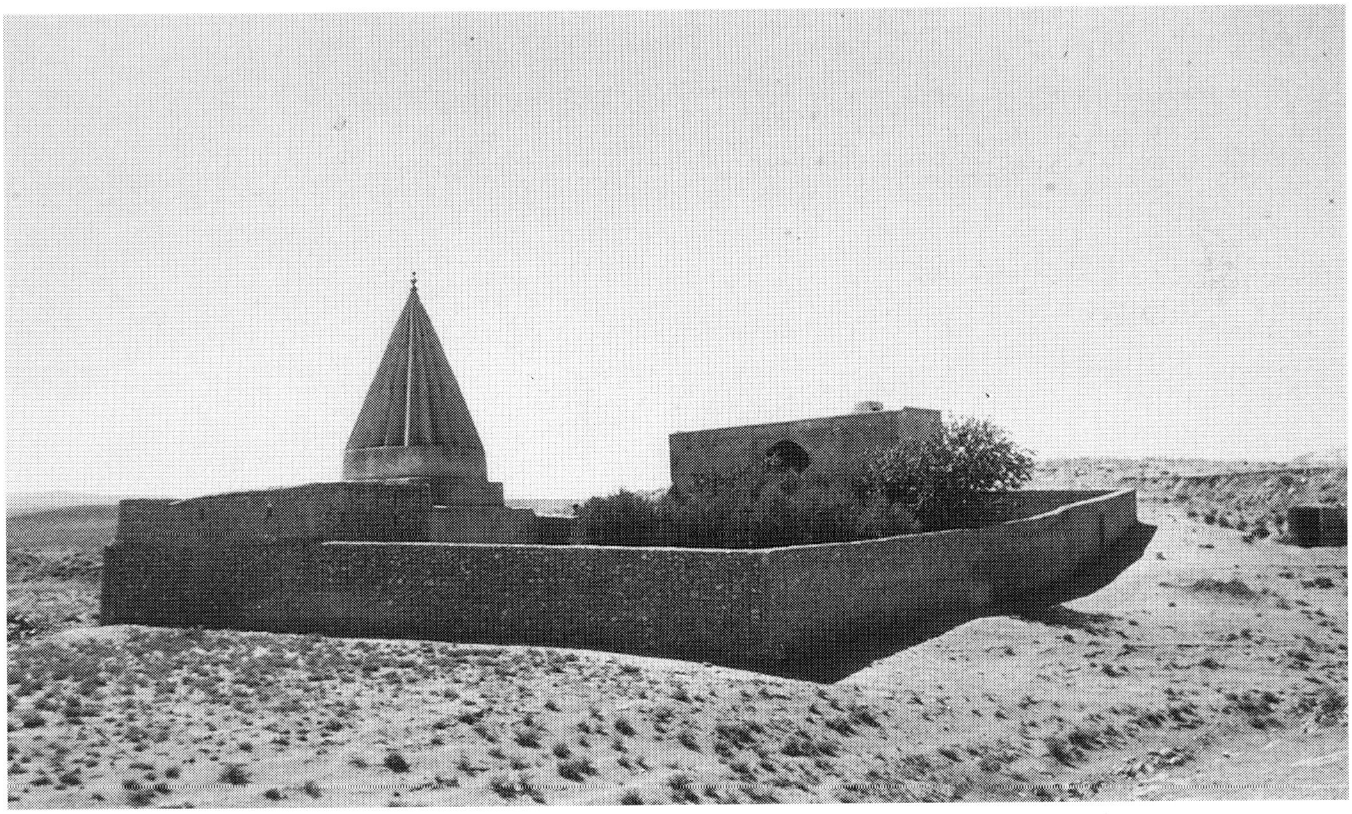

Yezidi Shrine near Mosul 1954

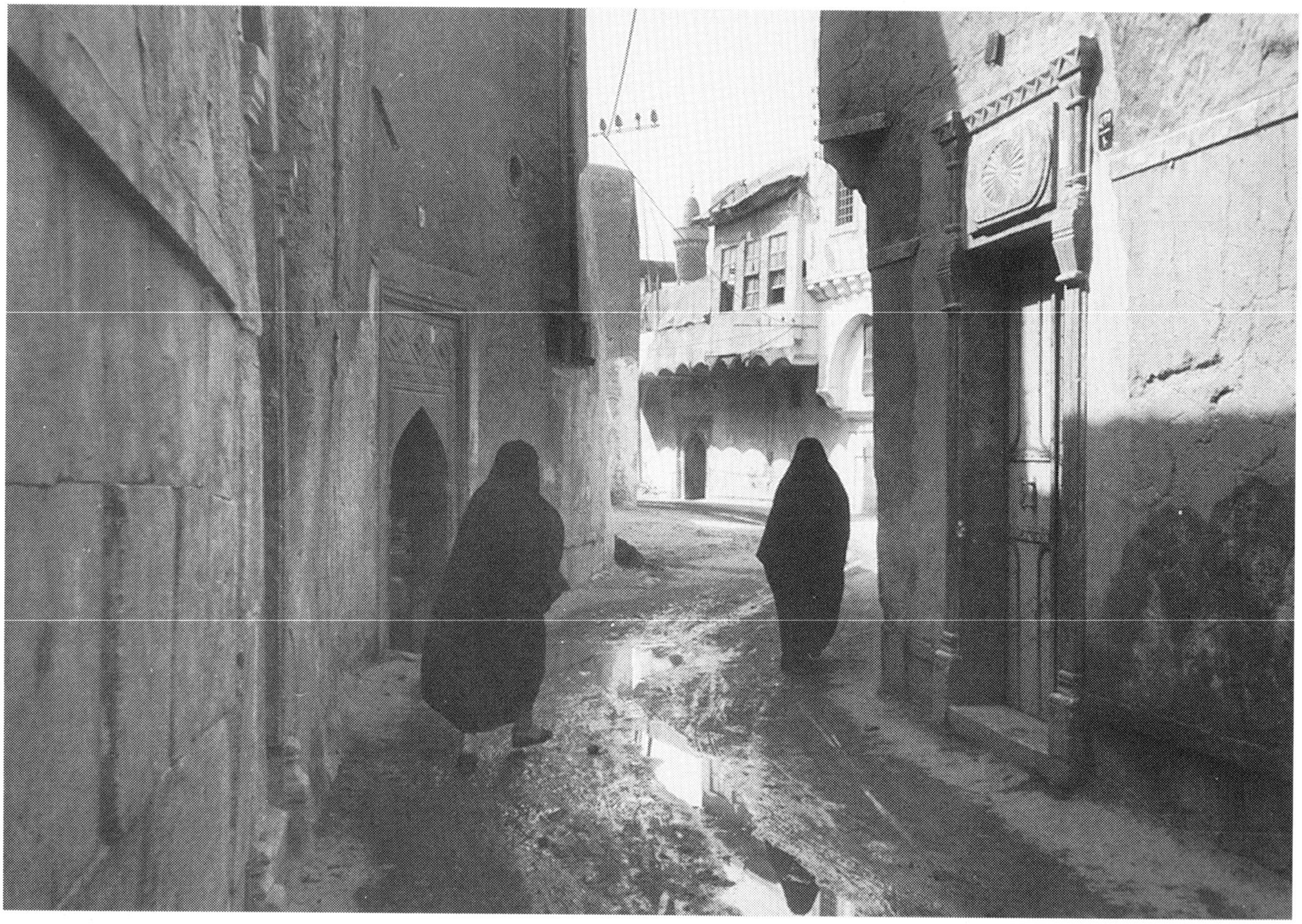

Mosul 1957

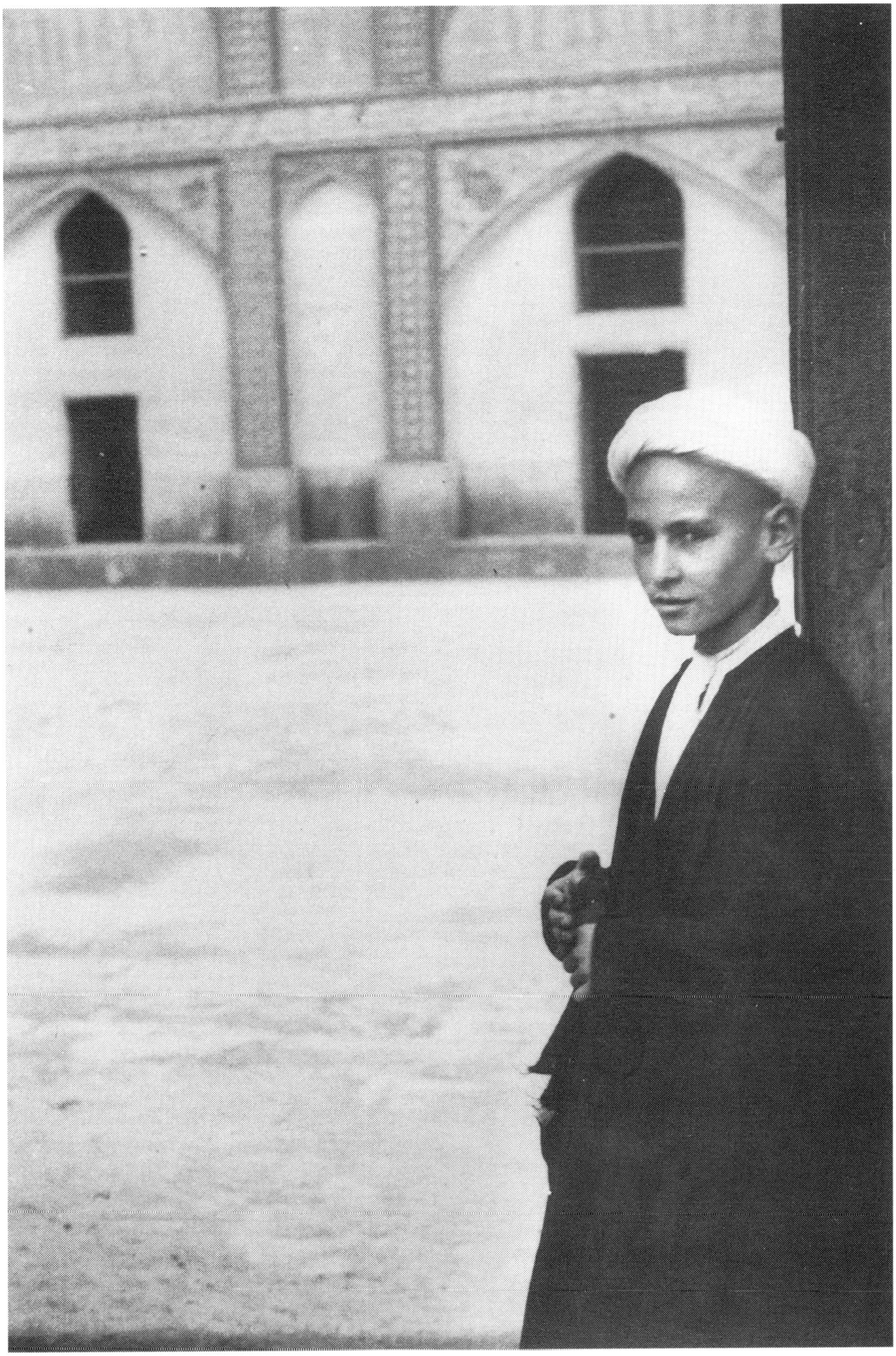

Samarra 1937

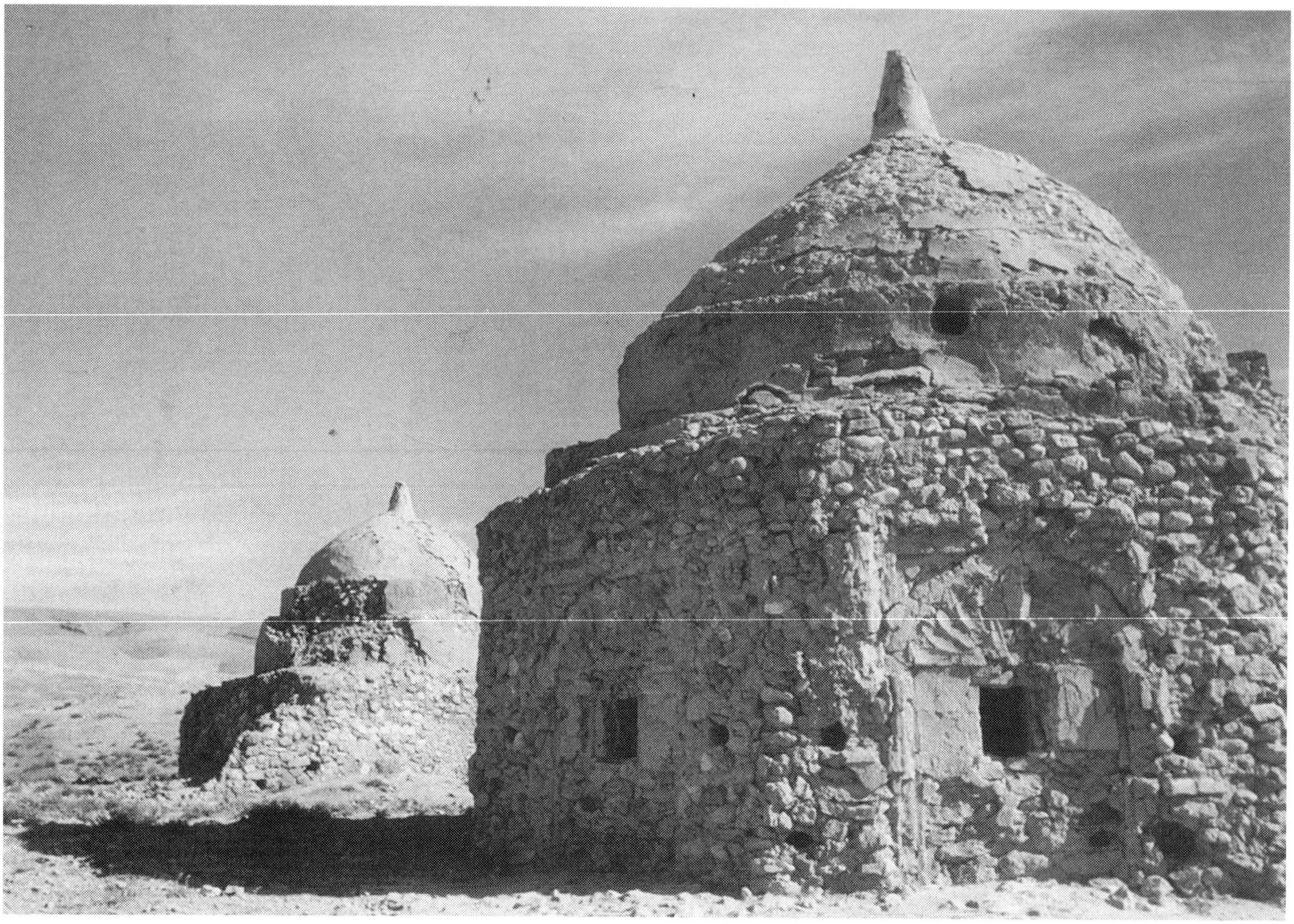

Tombs at Sinjar 1957

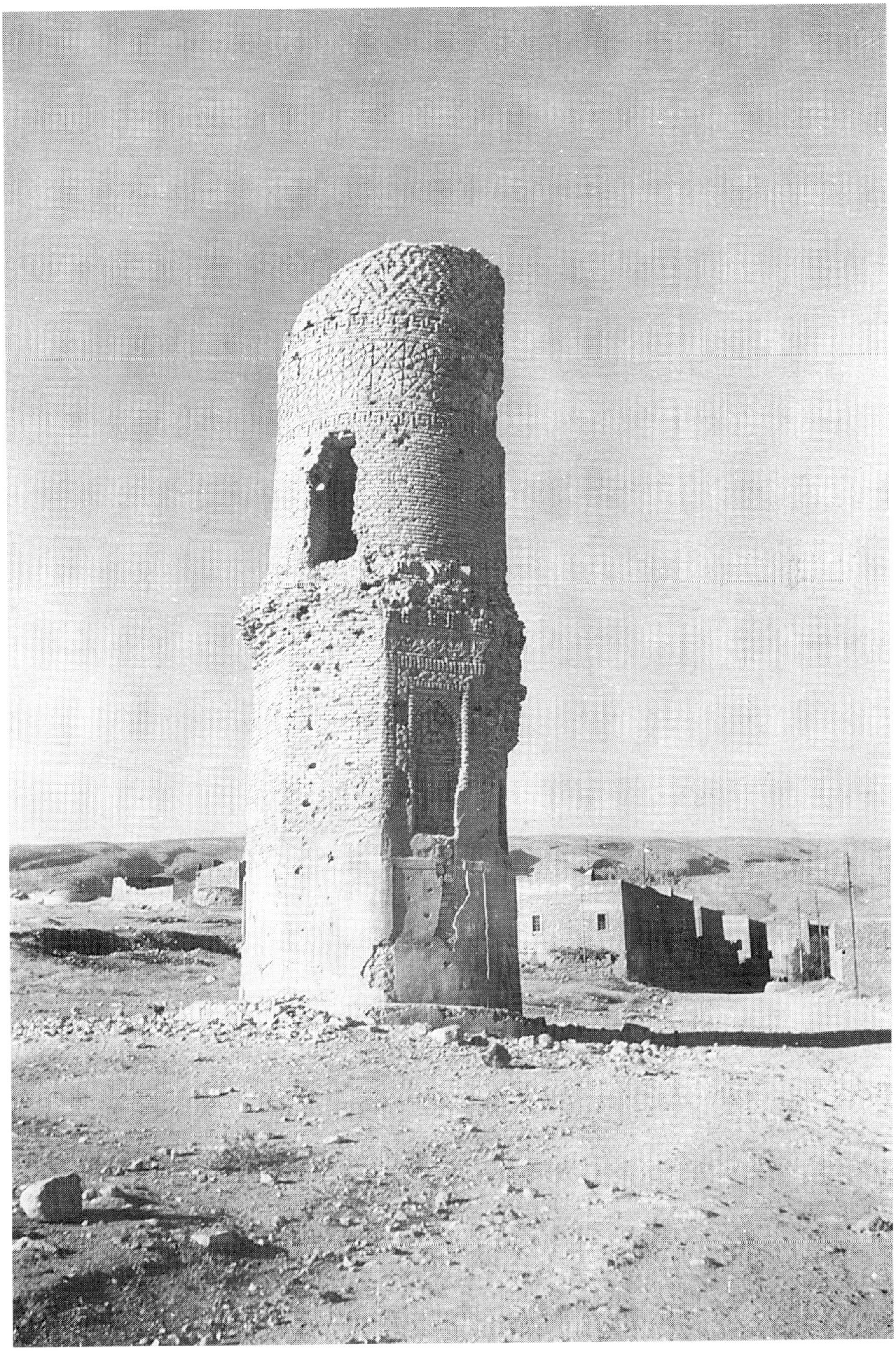

Minaret, Sinjar 1957

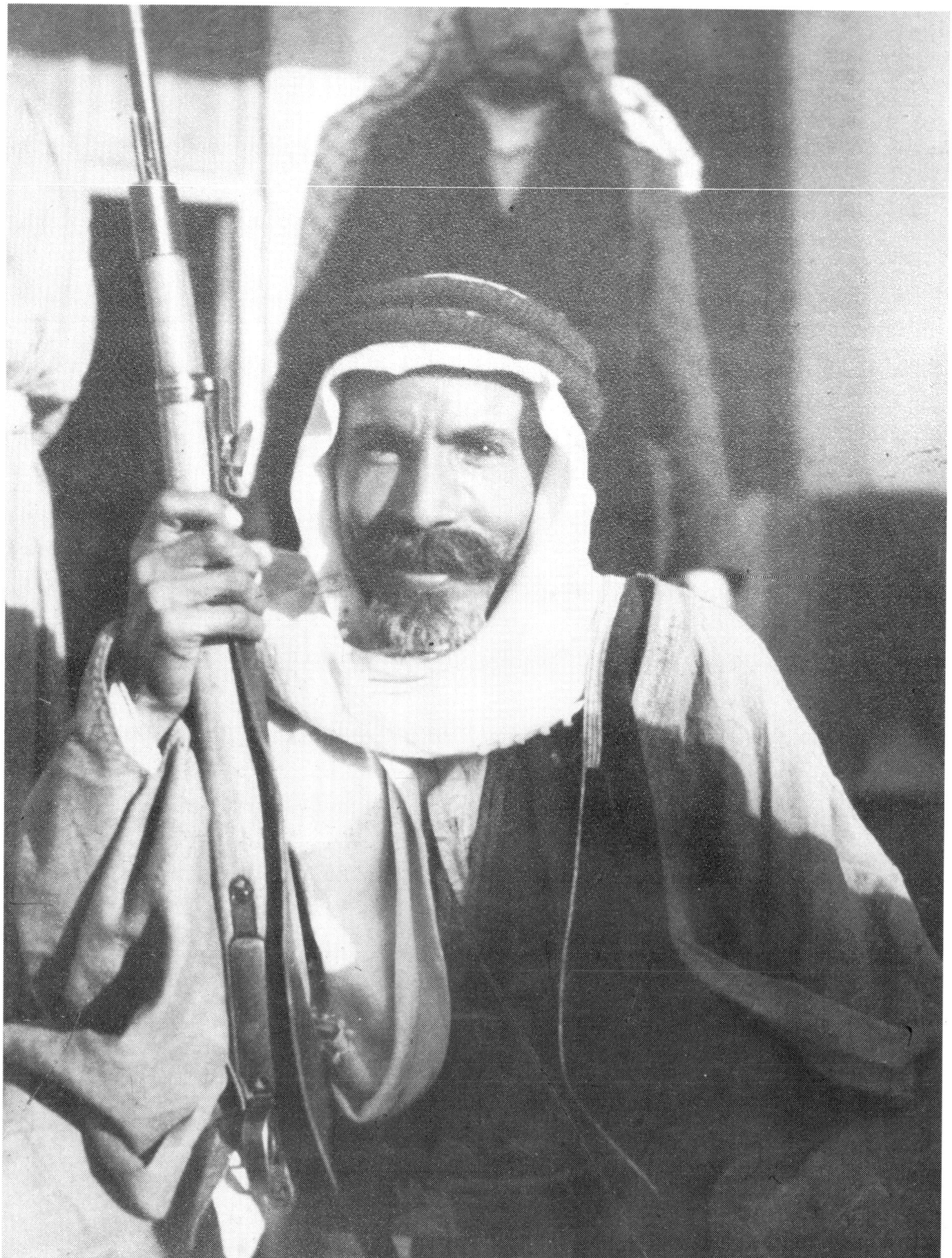

Aneiyah bedu 1954

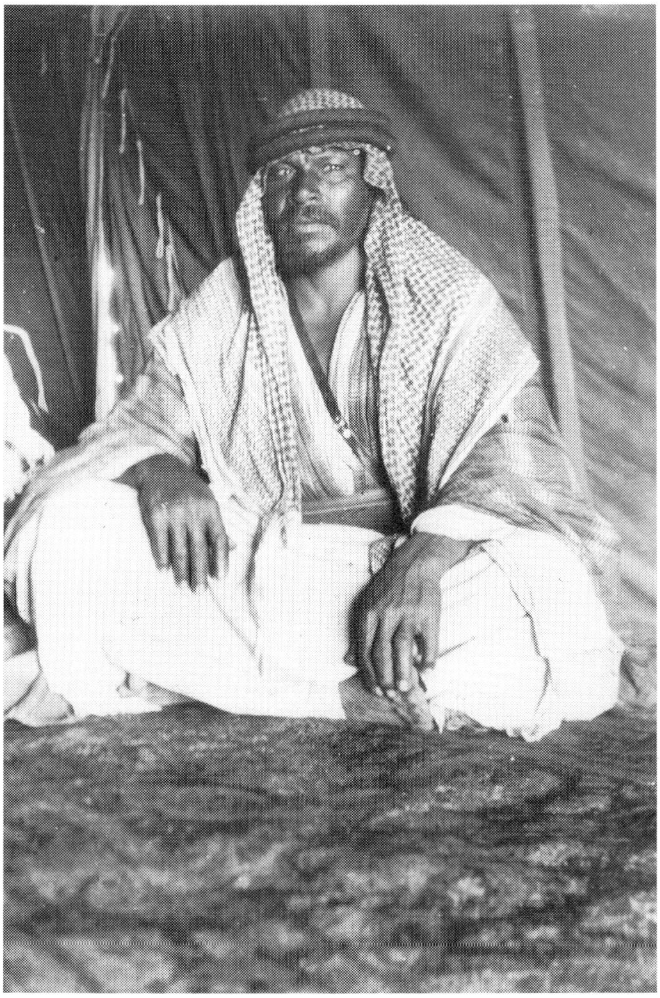

Shammar slave 1930

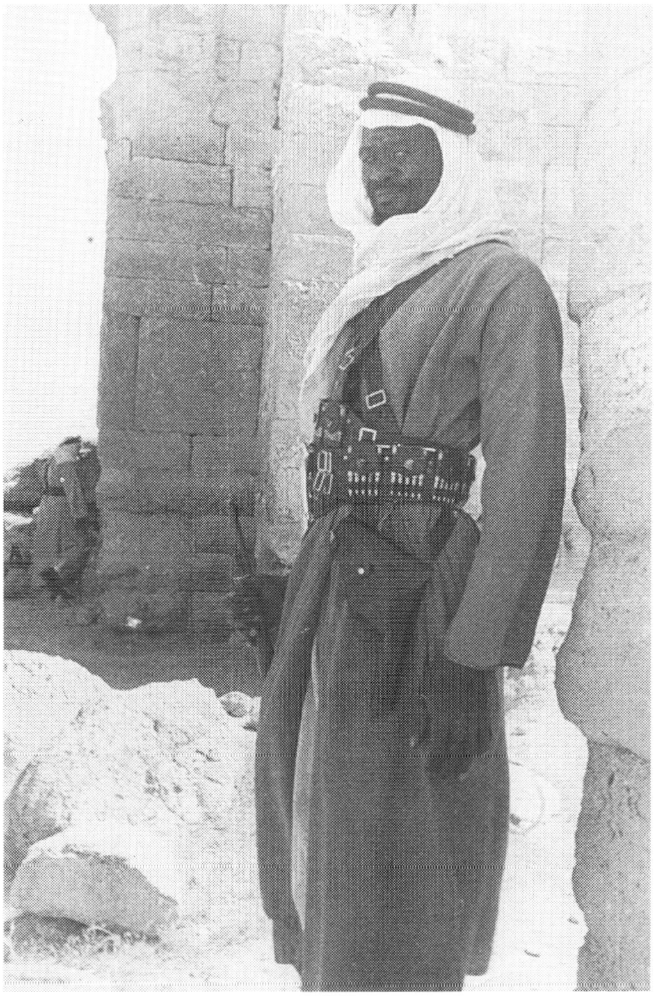

Slave guard, Hatra 1942

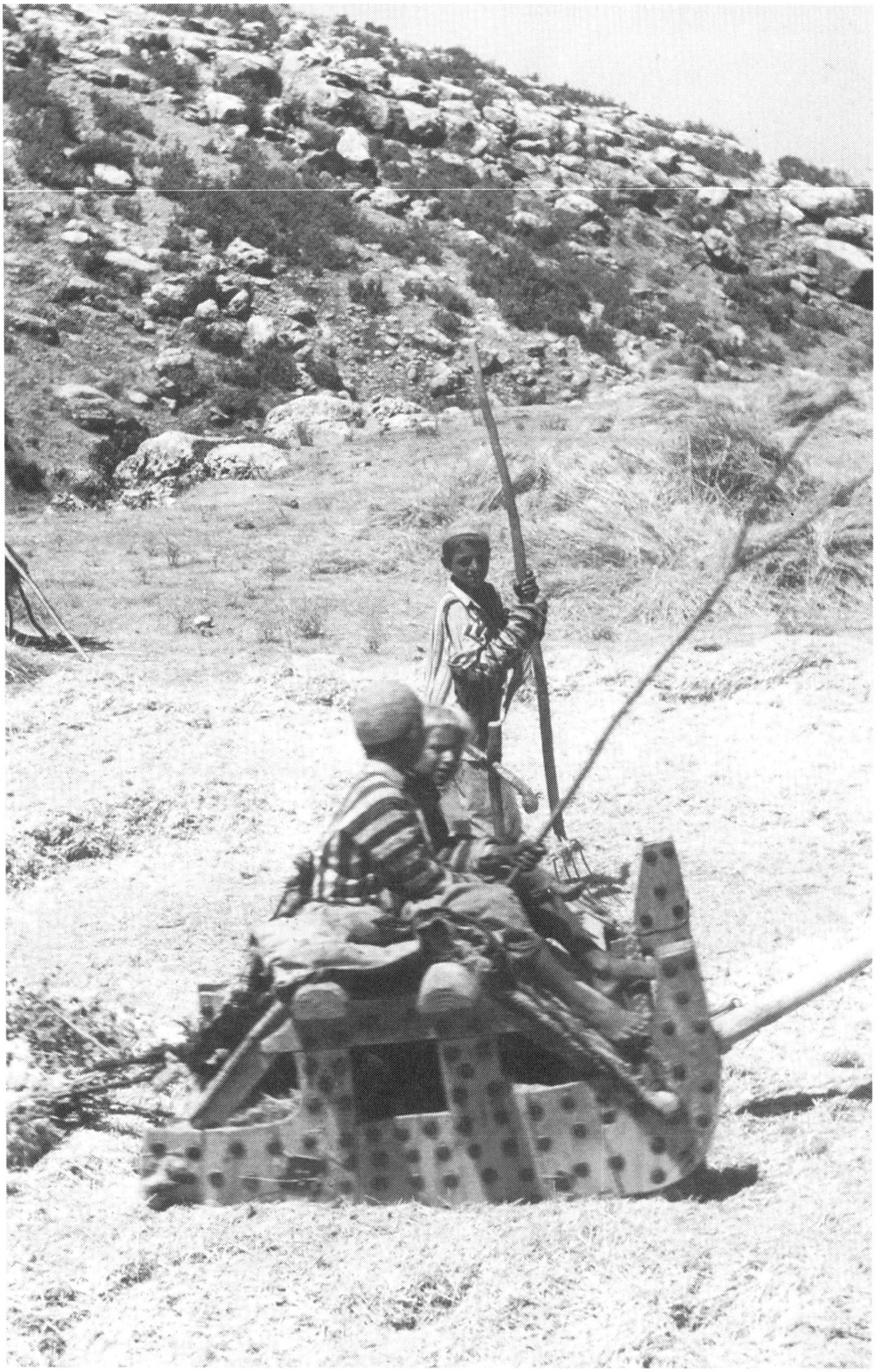

Threshing, Kurdistan 1954

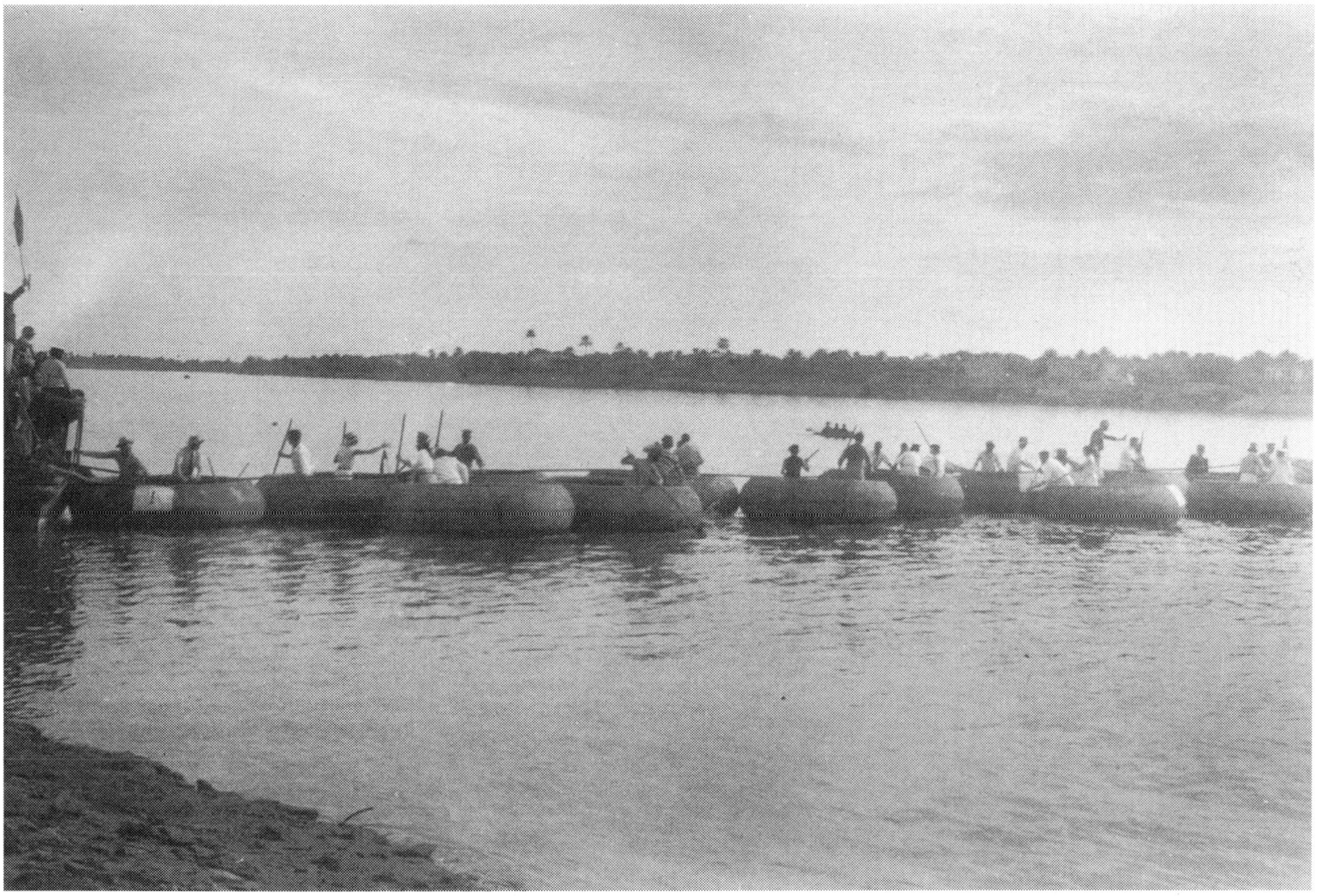

Gufa race on Tigris 1930. Gufas are "bowl-like coracles of woven basket coated with pitch".

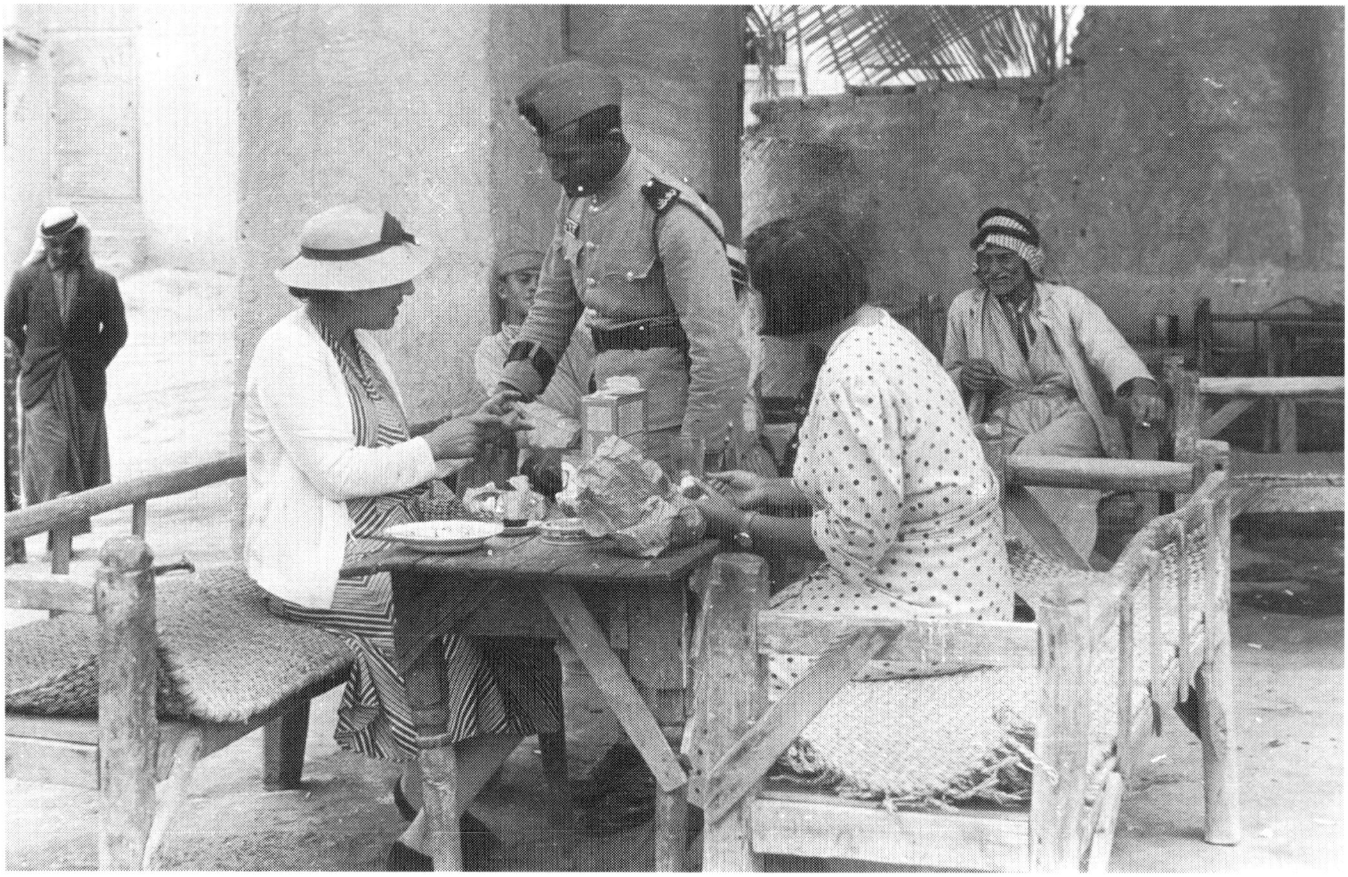

Stefana and Peggy Drower, Takrit 1937

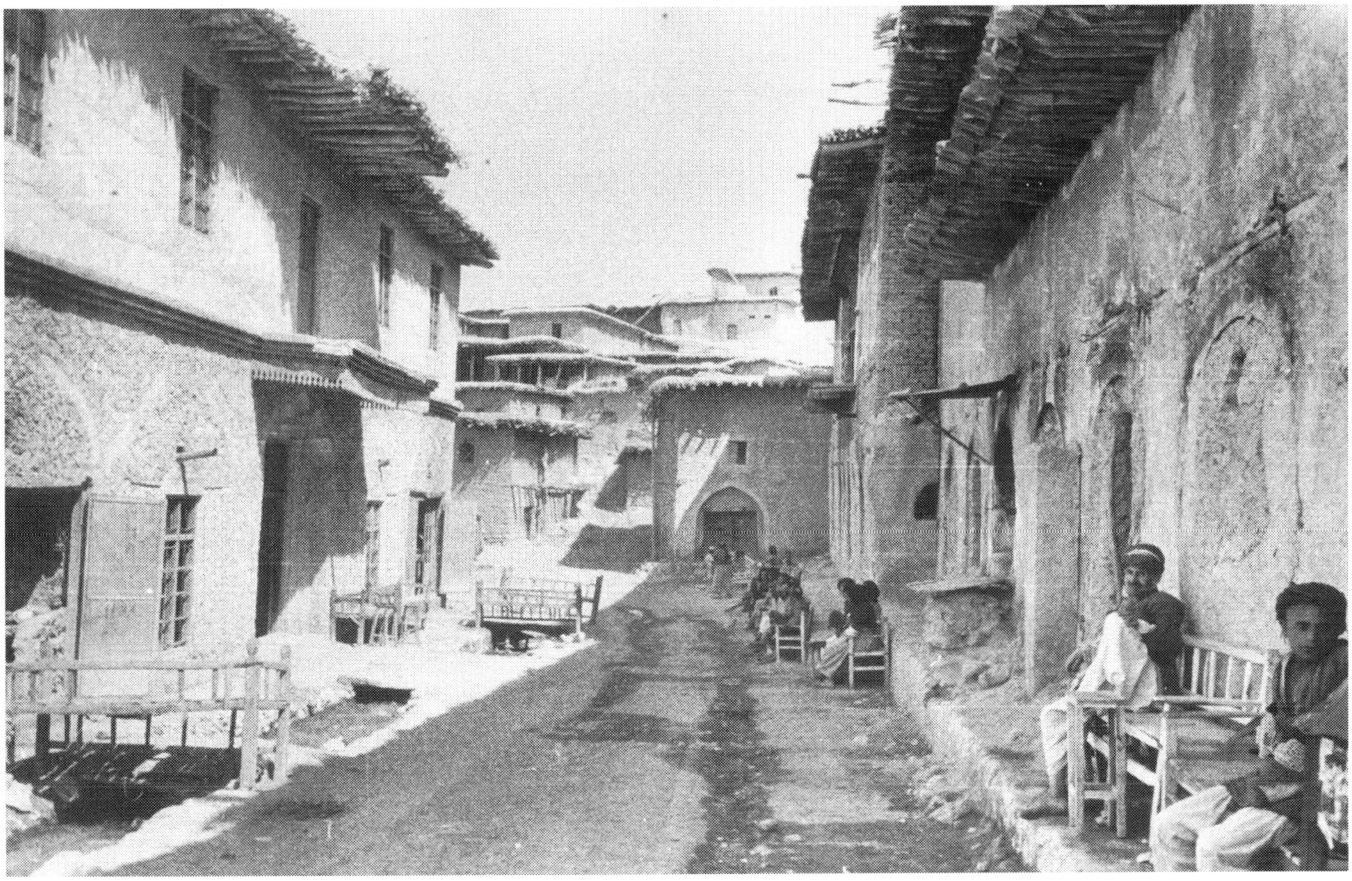

Chay Khana 1942

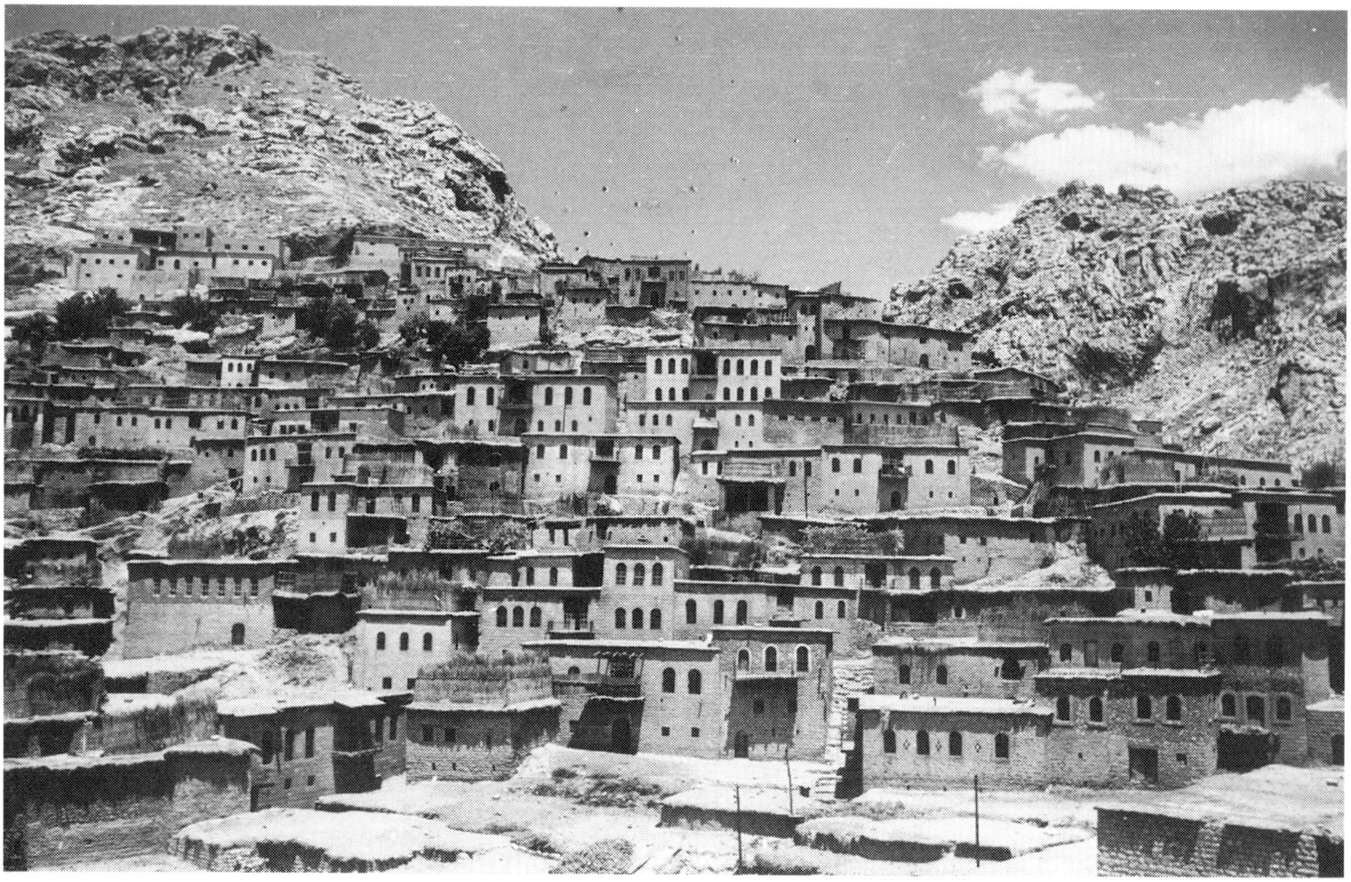

Aqrah, Kurdistan 1942

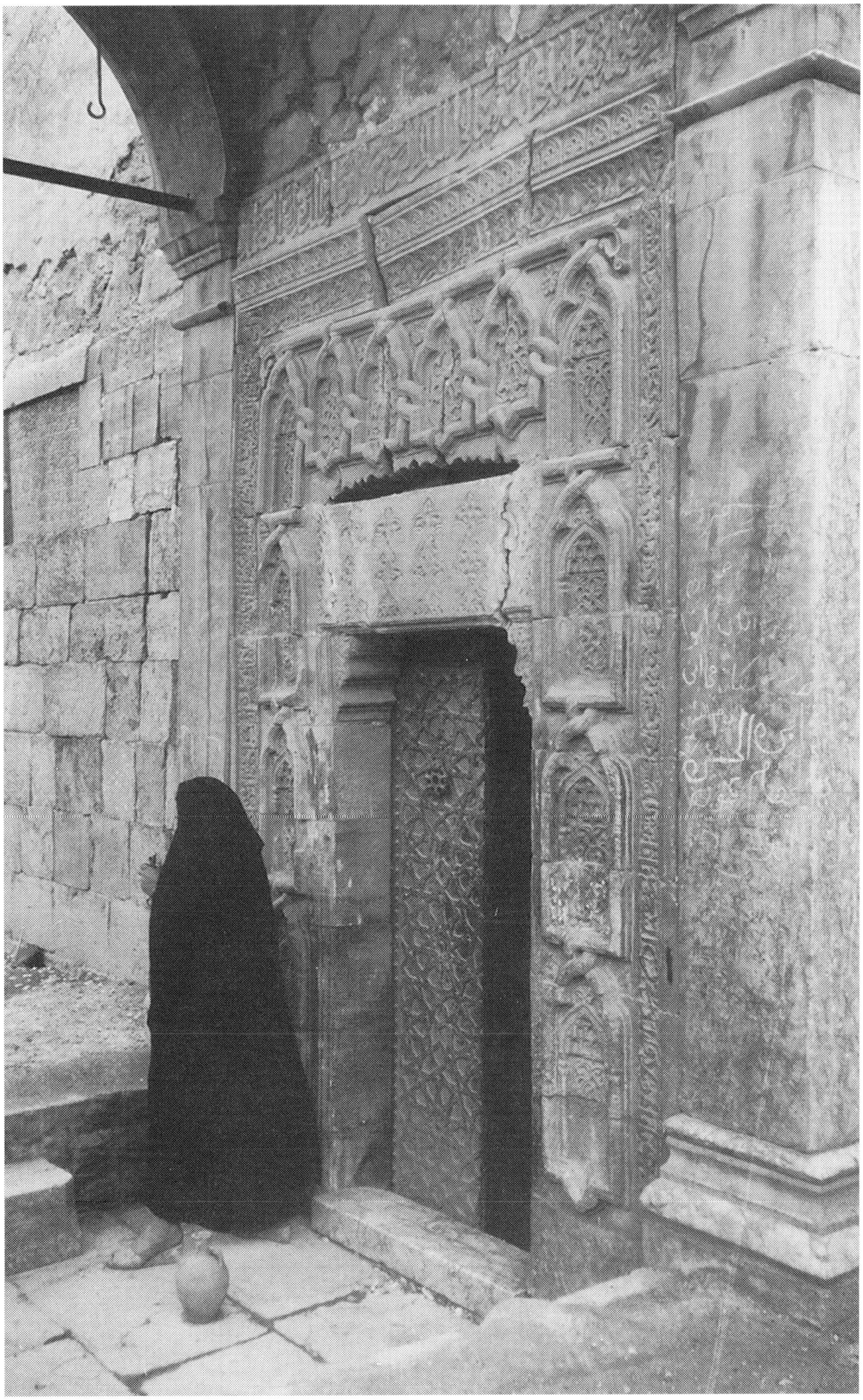

Mosul church 1954

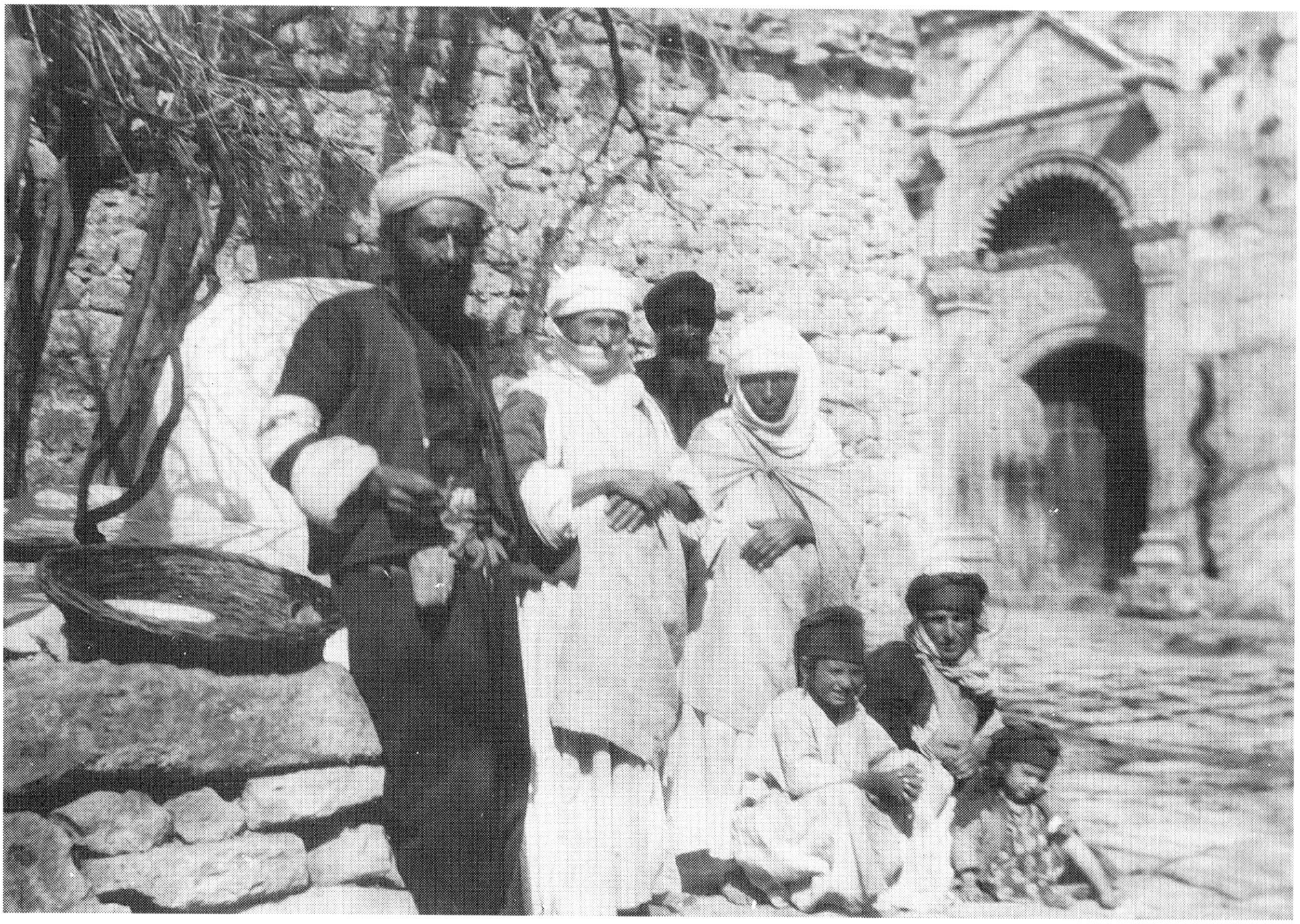

Yezidi priests, Sheikh 'Adi 1930. Note emblem of Satan attached to wall next to right-hand pillar.

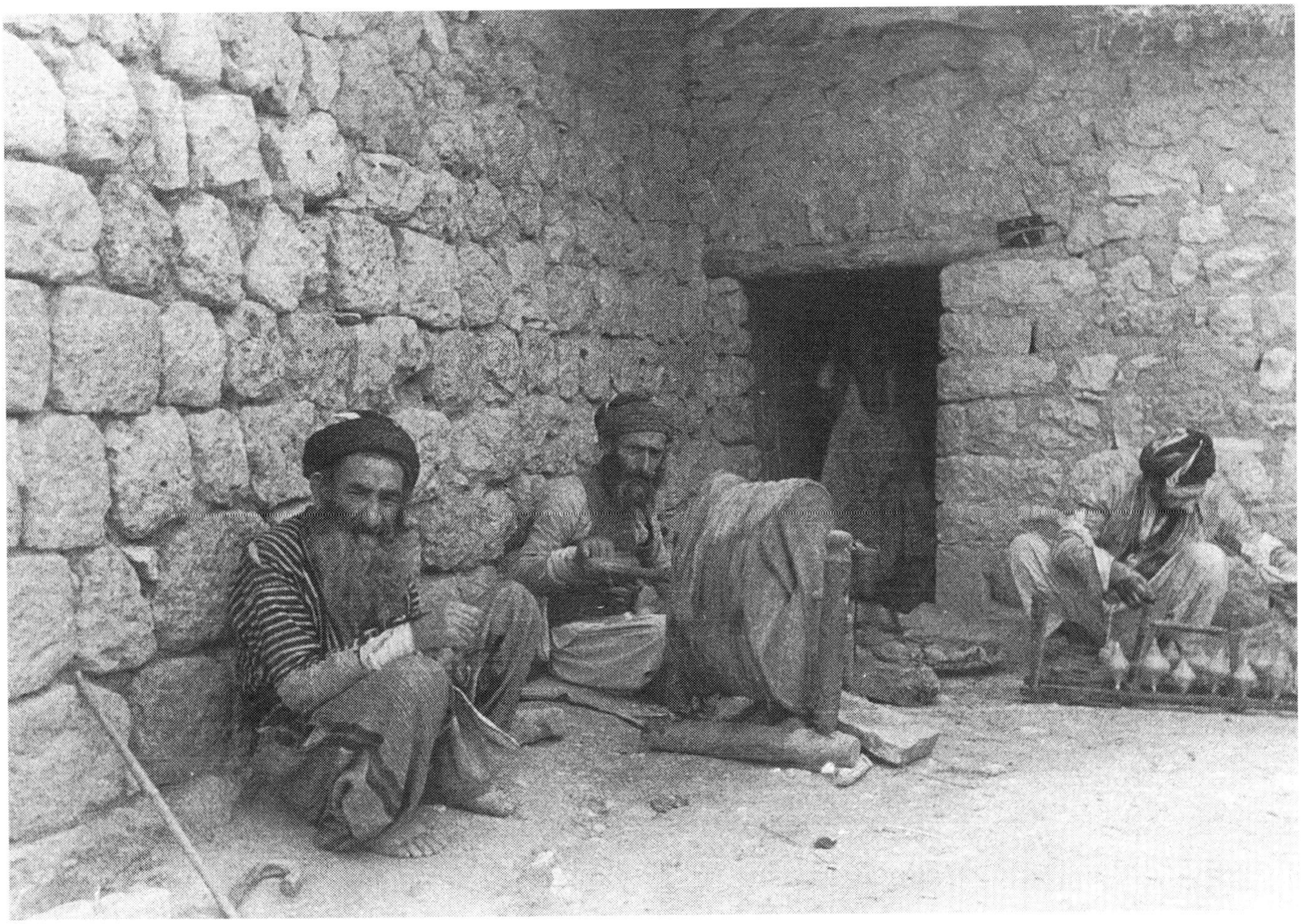

Jews in Amadiya, Kurdistan 1922

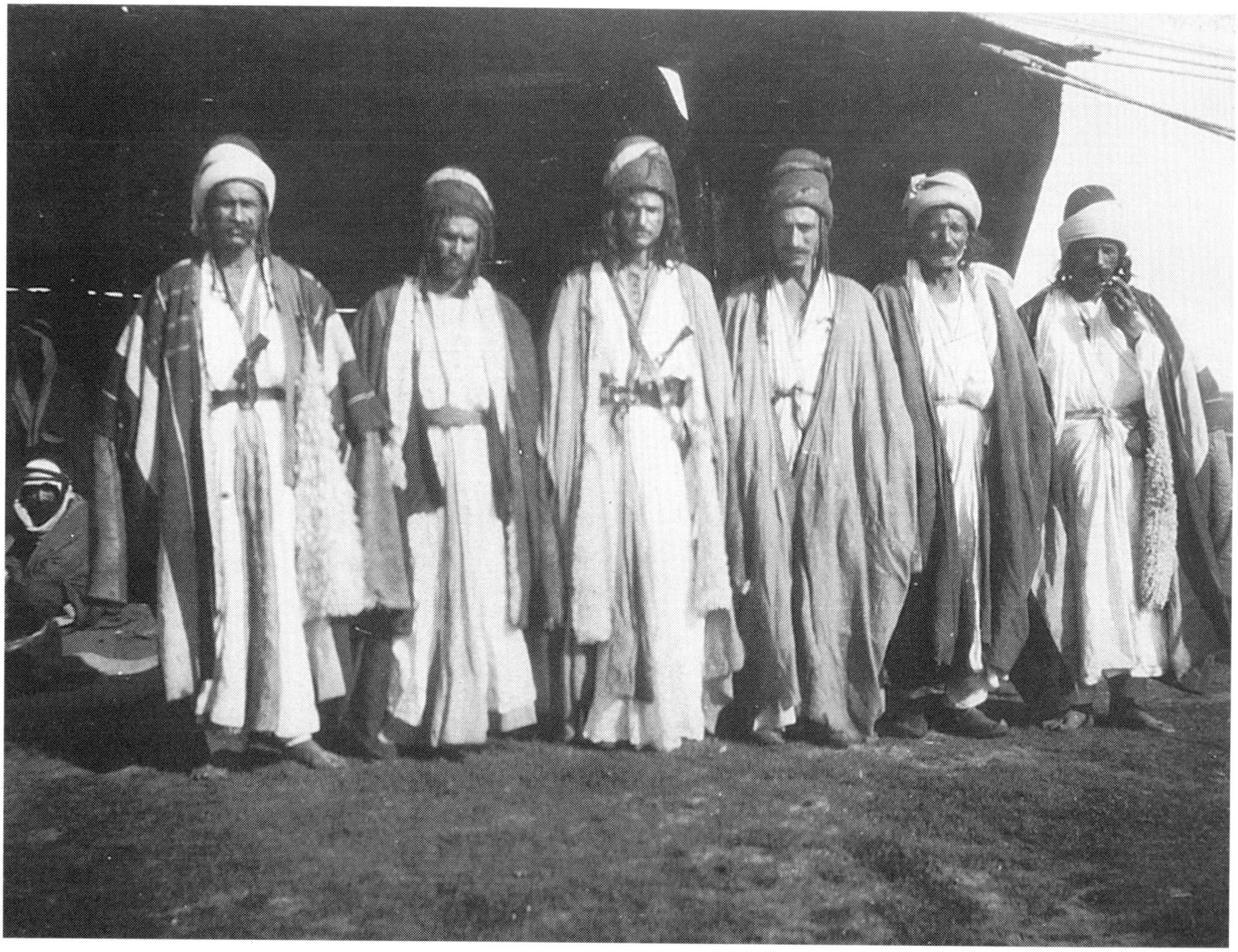

Yezidi guests of the Shammar 1930

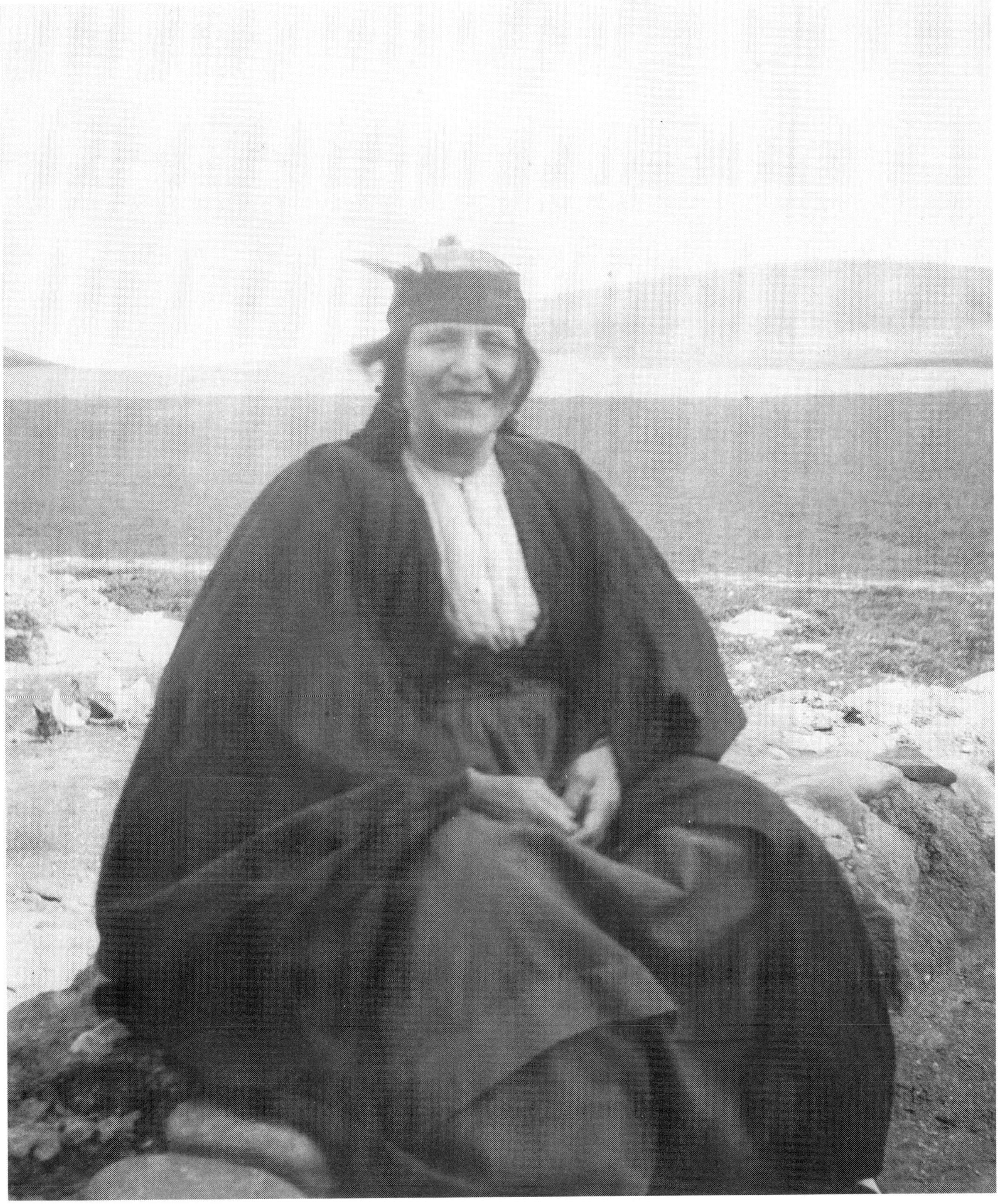

Chaldean woman at Mar Jirjis near Mosul 1930

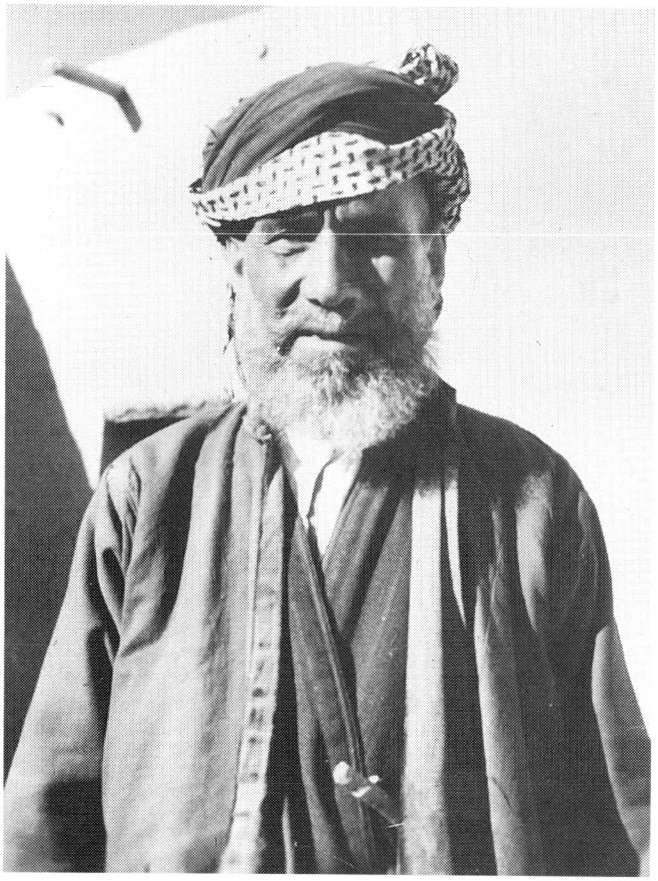

Tribesman, northern Iraq 1944

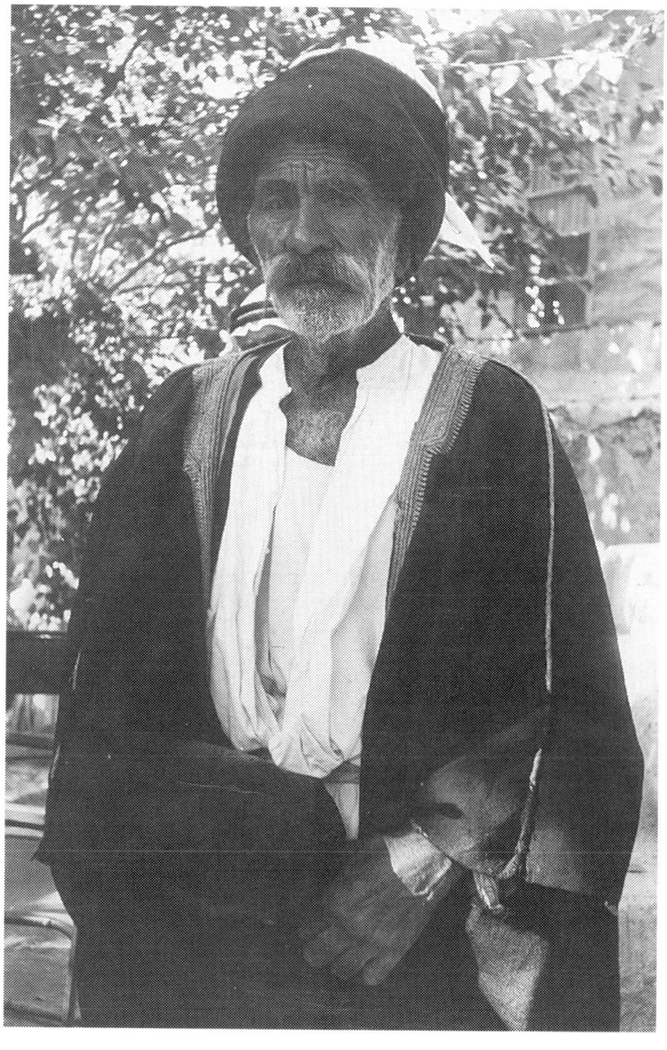

Yezidi *pir* (priest) 1957

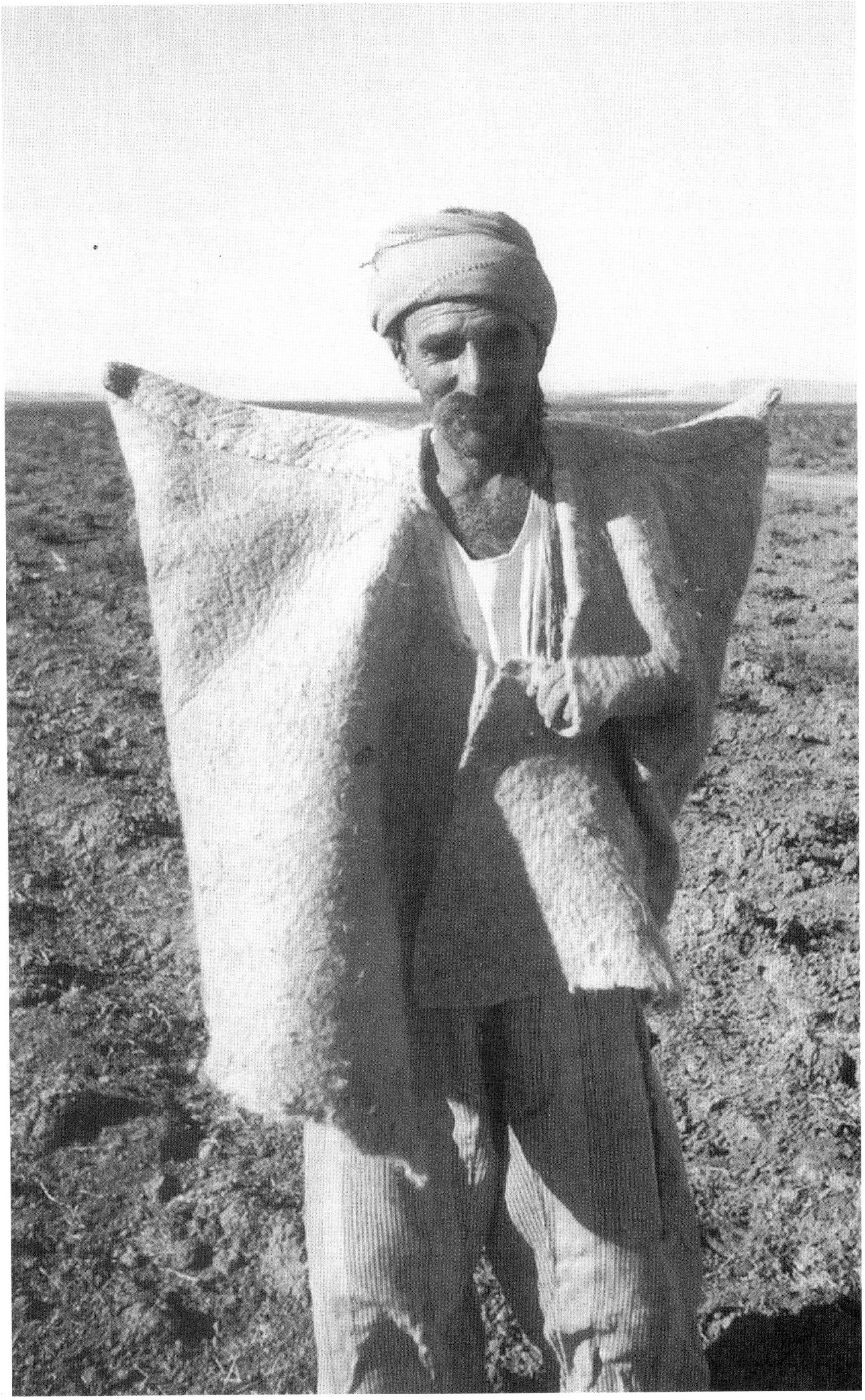

Shepherd at Fayshkhabur, near Zakho 1957

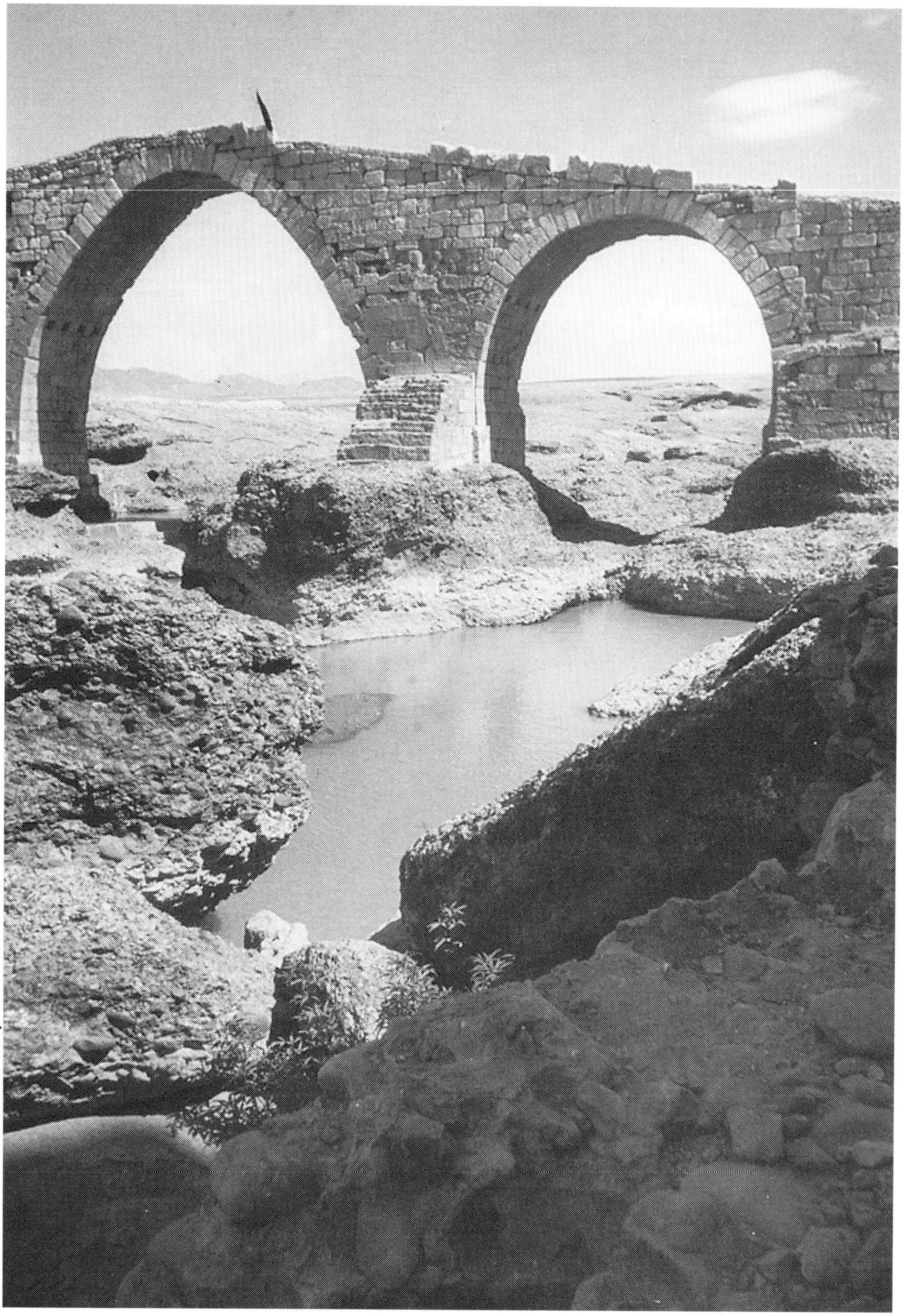

Zakho Bridge 1957

BAGHDAD

Freya's first encounter with Baghdad in 1929 was something of a shock: "What you see of the Caliphs' city is a most sordid aspect; a long low straight street, a dingy hybrid between East and West, with the unattractiveness of both. The crowd looks unhealthy and sallow, the children are pitiful, the shops are ineffective compromises with Europe; and the dust is wicked, for it turns to blood-poisoning at the slightest opportunity, and bears out the old Babylonian idea of an atmosphere inhabited by demons."

Through a contact in Damascus she found a lodging, for 1/6d (15p) a day in the older part of the city. The bustle and confusion soon fascinated her as she began to distinguish the individual trees from the wood. Her lodging, a tiny house in the narrowest of slums, proved insalubrious. When she complained of the smell of sewage that permeated the house from a holding tank under the floor, a British official found her a more pleasant billet among palm groves and "little Arab mud hovels" on the western side of the Tigris, opposite the old British Residency. Here, away from the smells, she could observe the life of the river.

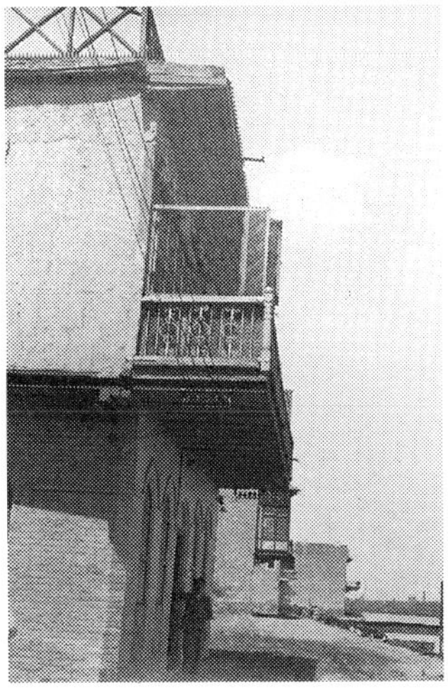

Freya Stark's house in Baghdad 1930

At Baghdad the River Tigris, fed by Armenian snows, is about three hundred metres wide. In 1930 the river was "the only sweet and fresh thoroughfare of the town". Along the paths lining its banks, barefoot women came to fill their water jars, and boatmen towed their vessels against the current. In the early mornings, when the mists hovered over its swirling eddies, or at eventide, when the sunset sent yellow shafts through the haze and dust, water buffaloes came down to drink. The traffic spanned four thousands of years of river navigation: *gufas*, pitch-coated coracles of woven basket, *shashturs*, long rectangular barges similar to those depicted in Assyrian sculptures and *kiliks*, rafts consisting simply of planks roped together and buoyed on inflated goatskins, were among the most ancient of craft; the British High Commissioner's launch and the steamers bringing American tourists or pilgrims from the holy cities of Najaf and Kerbala spoke for the twentieth century.

Freya's sympathy for the traditional order extended to the people lower down the social scale who, while living in the city, held to local customs of speech, manners and dress. Compared to the European city, with its long history of corporate autonomy, the Middle East city was a collection of villages, consisting of a mosaic of ethnic and religious affiliations. Every quarter and every sect had a different style of speech and manner of dress. Sunnis wore the red and white *keffiyeh* (head covering); the Shia version was black and white. Sayyids, who claimed descent from the Prophet, wore green turbans. The Indian, Jewish and Armenian merchants, and their women, wore their own distinctive costumes, each differentiated, to the knowledgeble eye, by subtleties of material and fold. The newly proletarianized Kurds and Lurs (from Luristan in Western Persia) who acted as porters in the alleys and thoroughfares that were too narrow for wheeled traffic, could be distinguished by their country clothes.

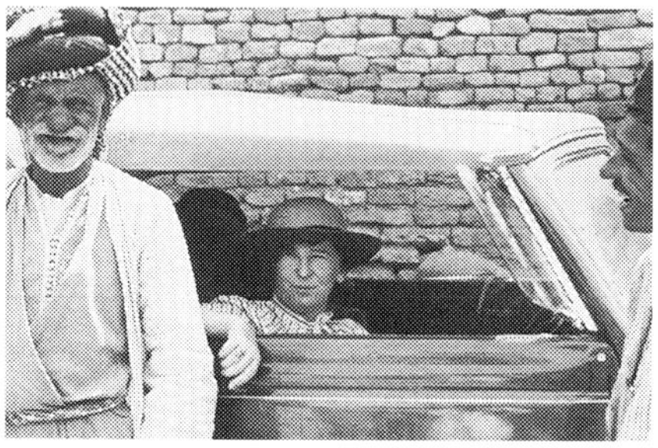

Freya Stark in Baghdad 1941

After the Second World War the dark bazaars and narrow alleys began to vanish under the rectilinear contours of the modern metropolis. Freya did not regret their passing. "A new and rather exciting Baghdad is growing," she told her friend and mentor Sir Sydney Cockerell in 1954. "The modern cubist shapes with straight undecorated lines I think *suit* this country; and there is a band of young architects and artists . . . who are working in the brick that was the only thing the Baghdad builders really learned to deal with."

Freya made her last visit to Baghdad in September 1957. She spent "two perfect days" there staying with friends. It was, she said, "like walking back into my youth and dreams". She admired the bright new shops, the "brittle shining luxuries and huge American taxis" and had an audience with the King, who talked of his plans for his people, the new palace he was building and his forthcoming marriage. Within ten months he was dead, killed in a shoot-out between revolutionary soldiers and the palace guard.

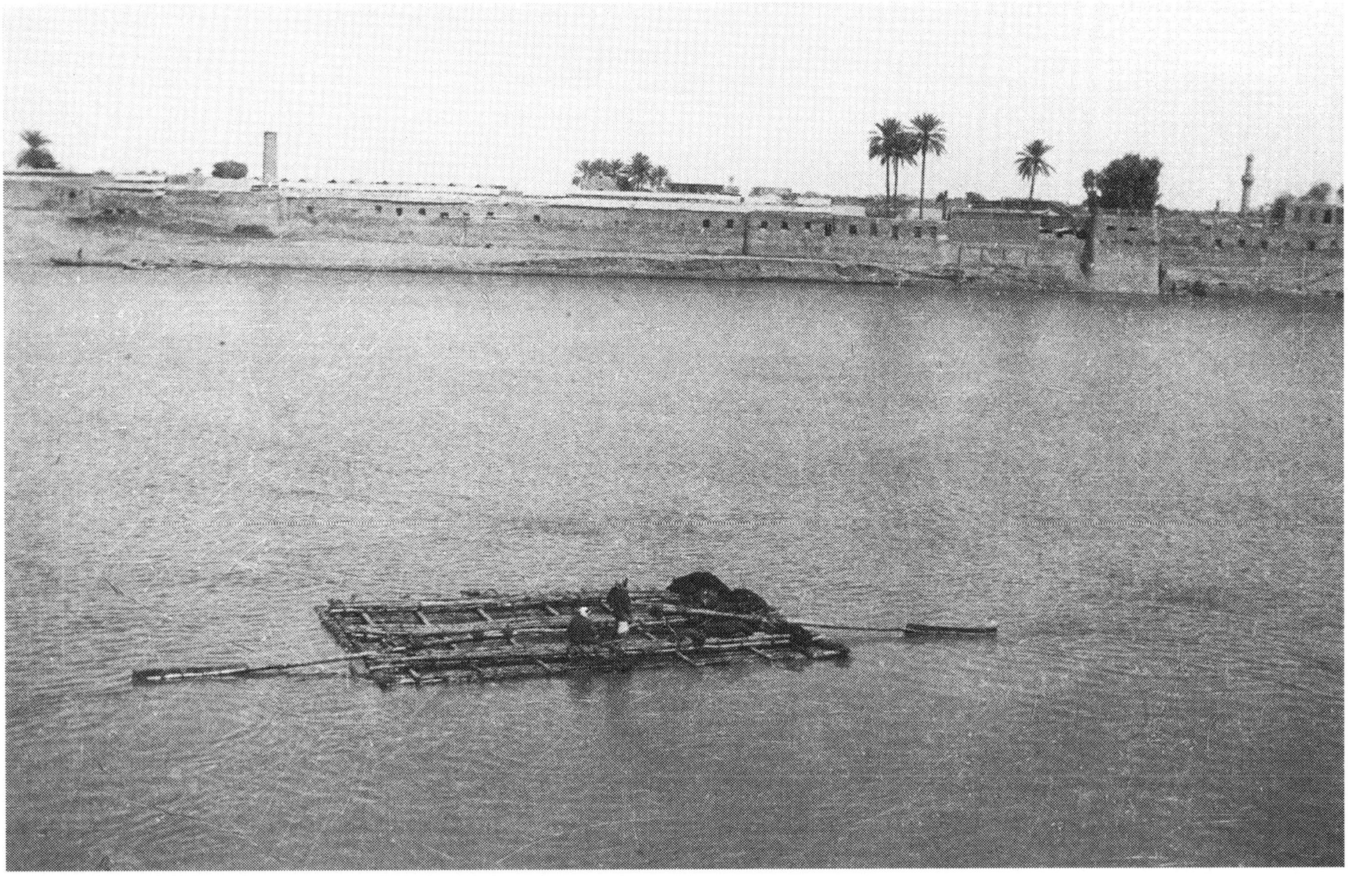

"Kilik" on the Tigris above Baghdad 1937

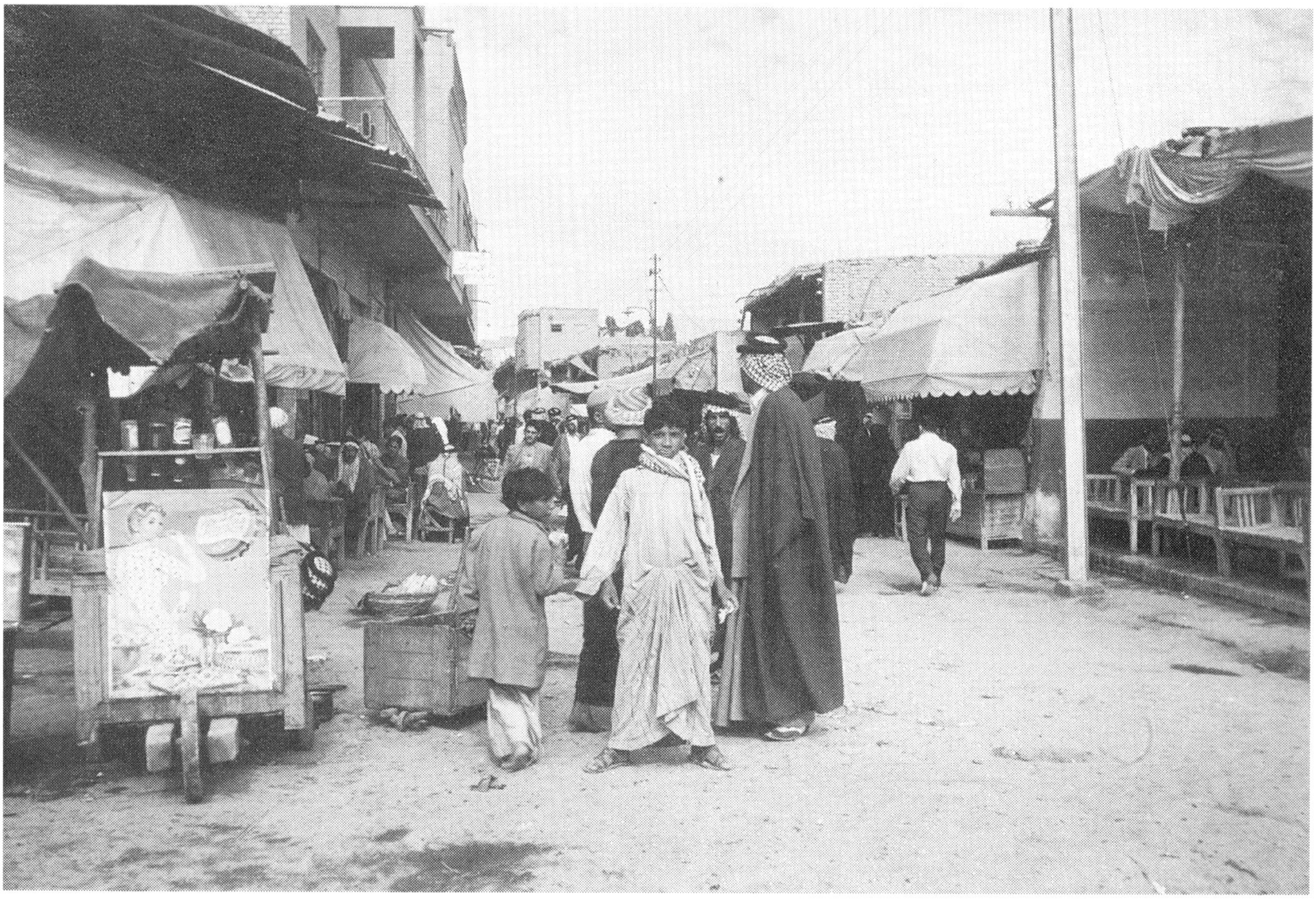

Baghdad suburb 1957

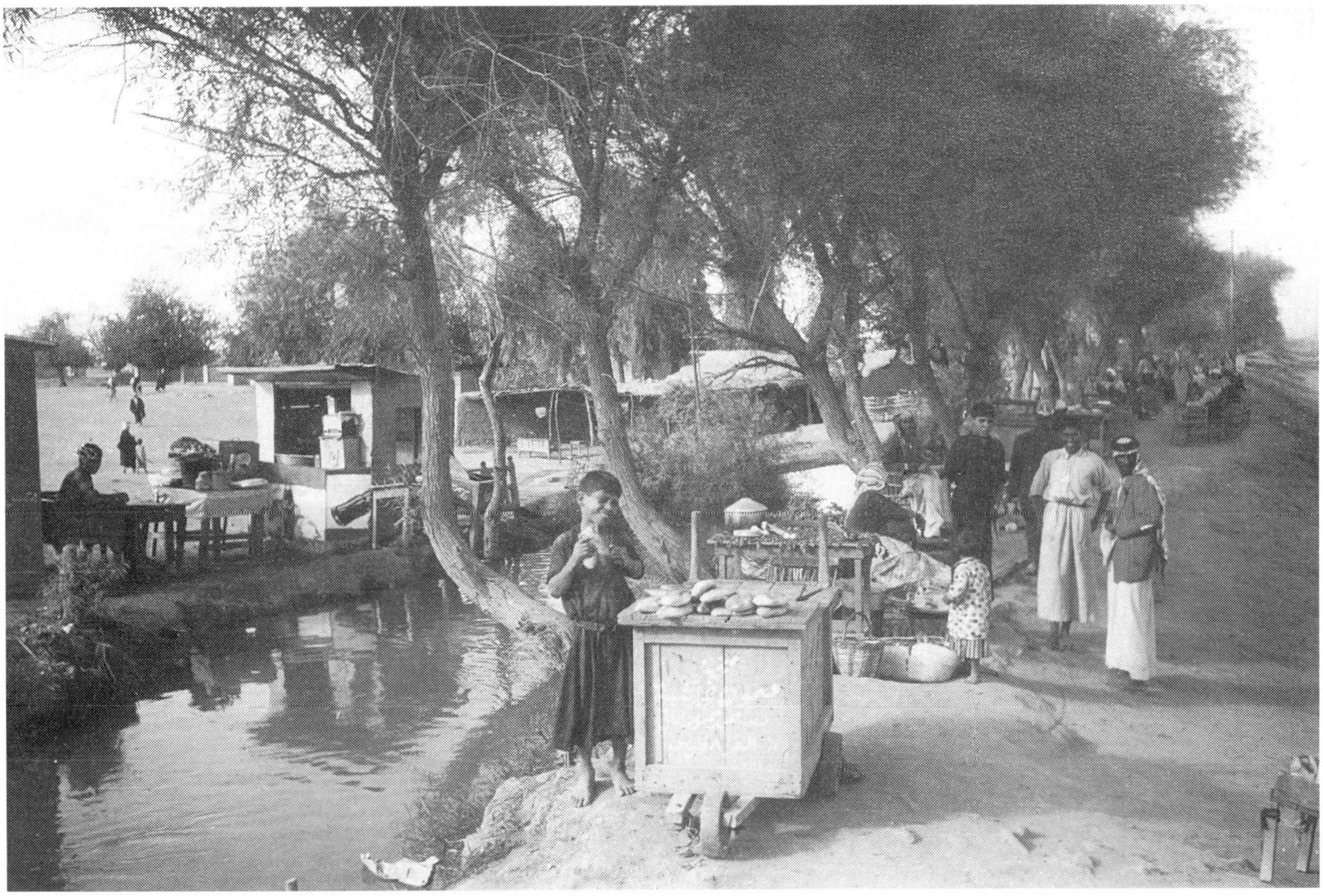

Baghdad suburb 1957

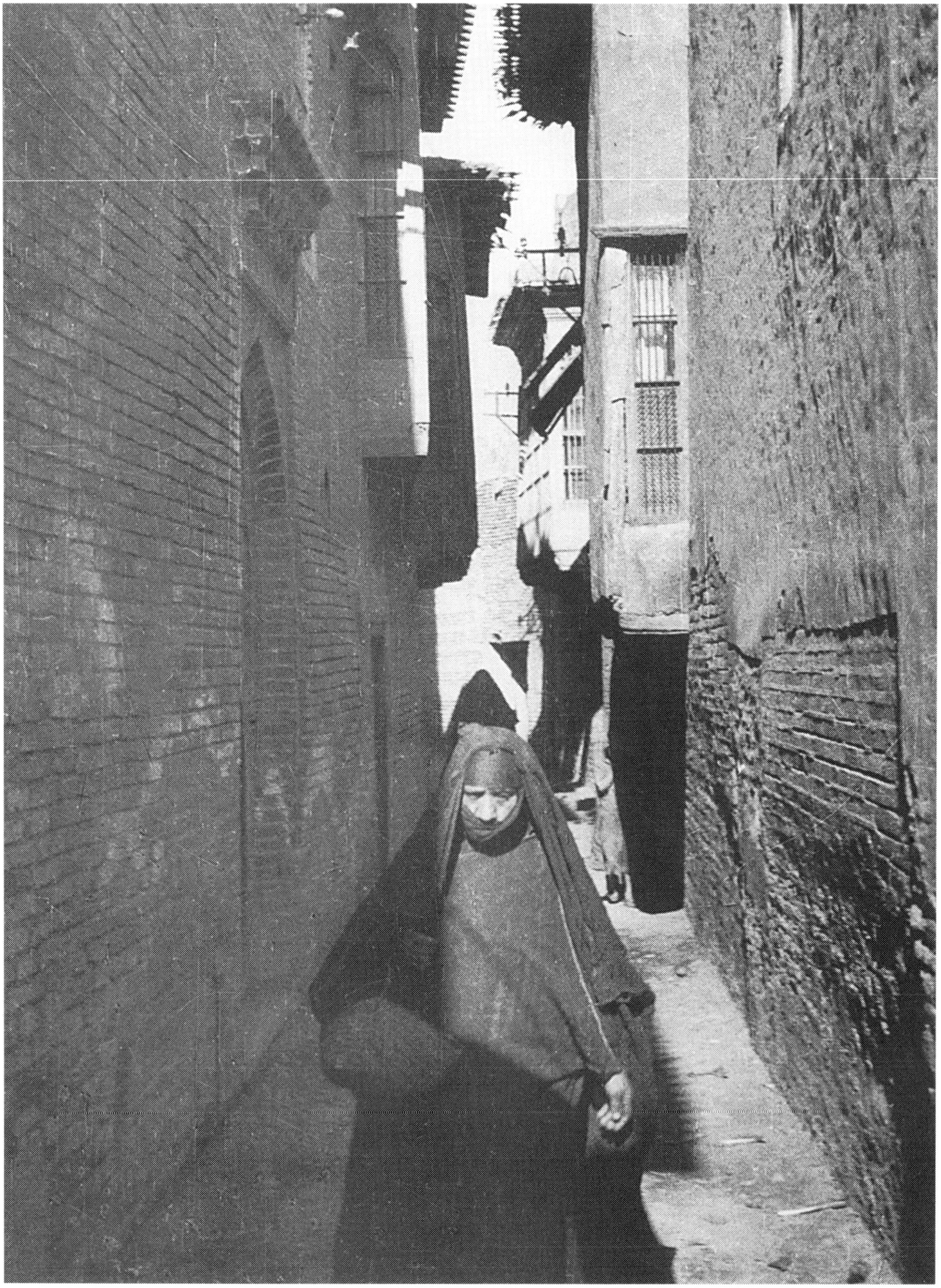

Baghdad street 1941

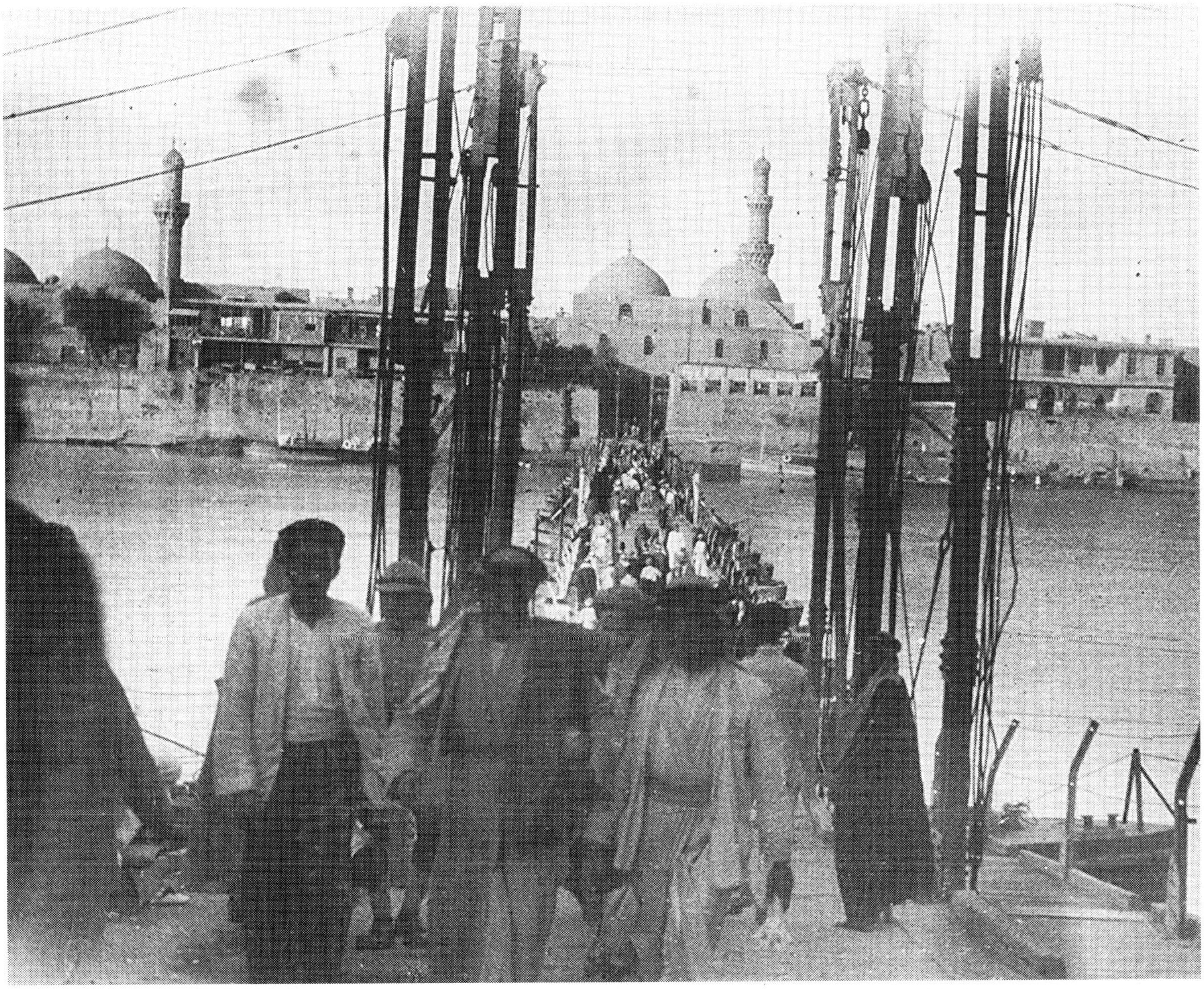

Pontoon bridge 1930

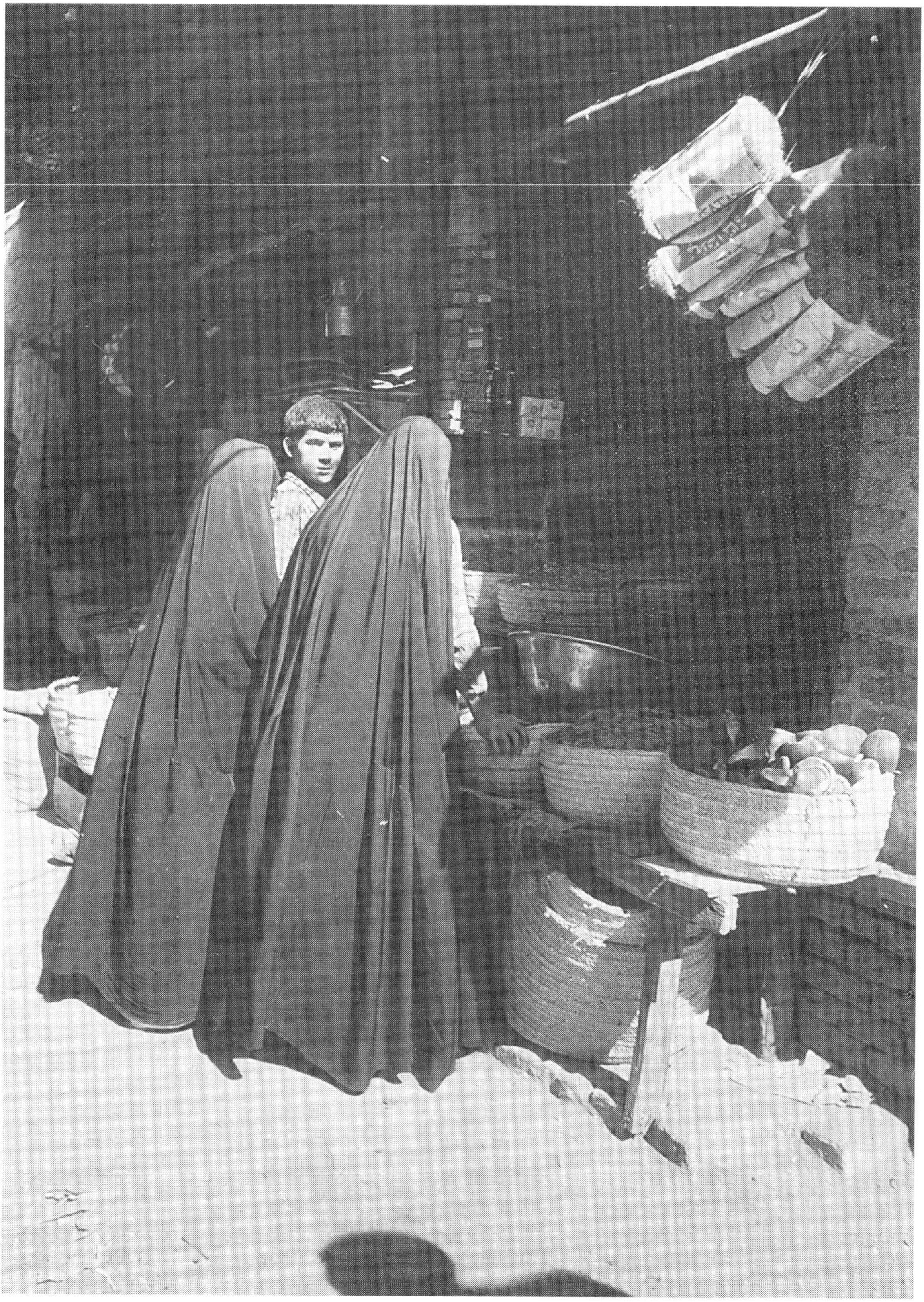

Market scene 1937

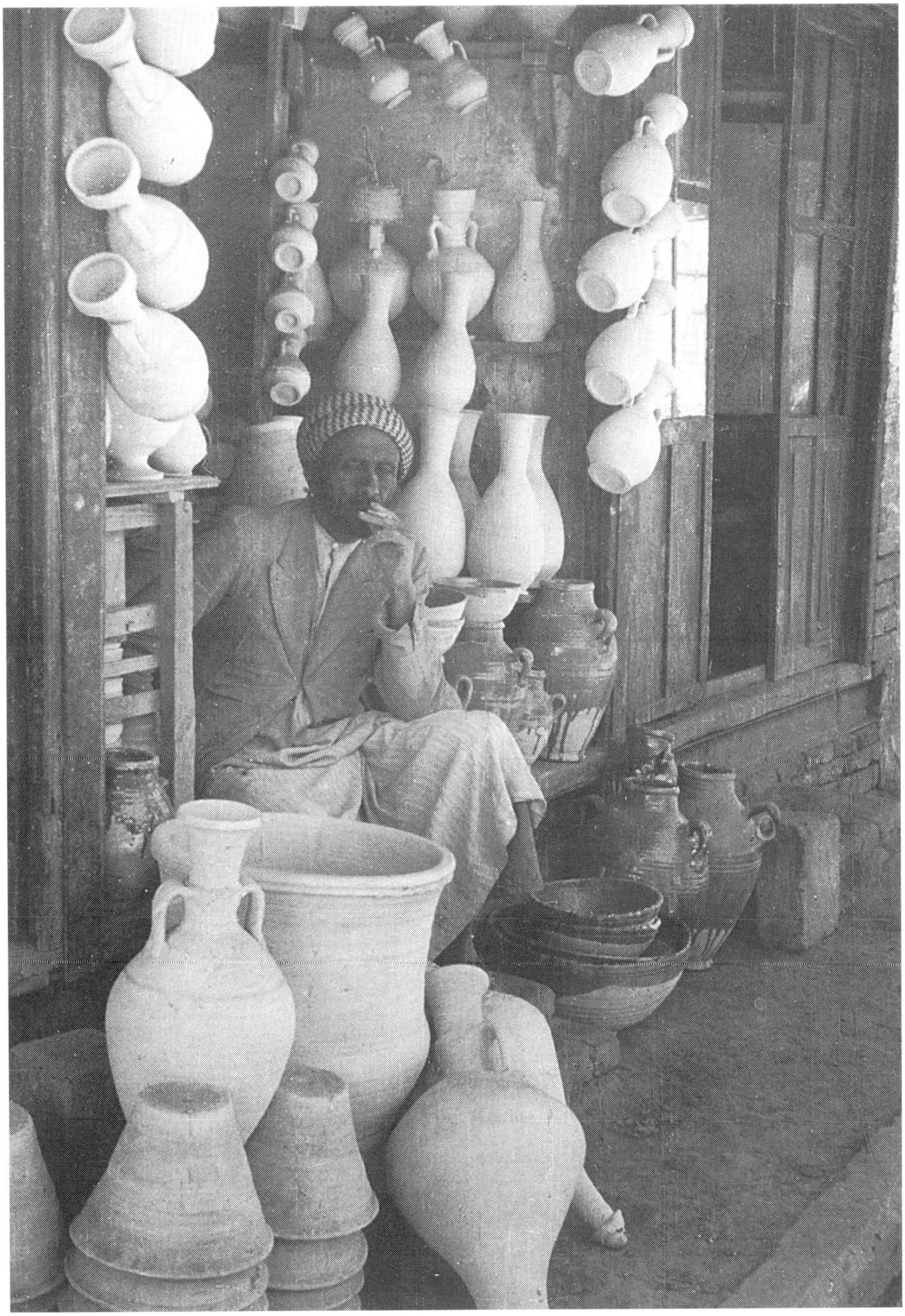

Potter and his wares 1937

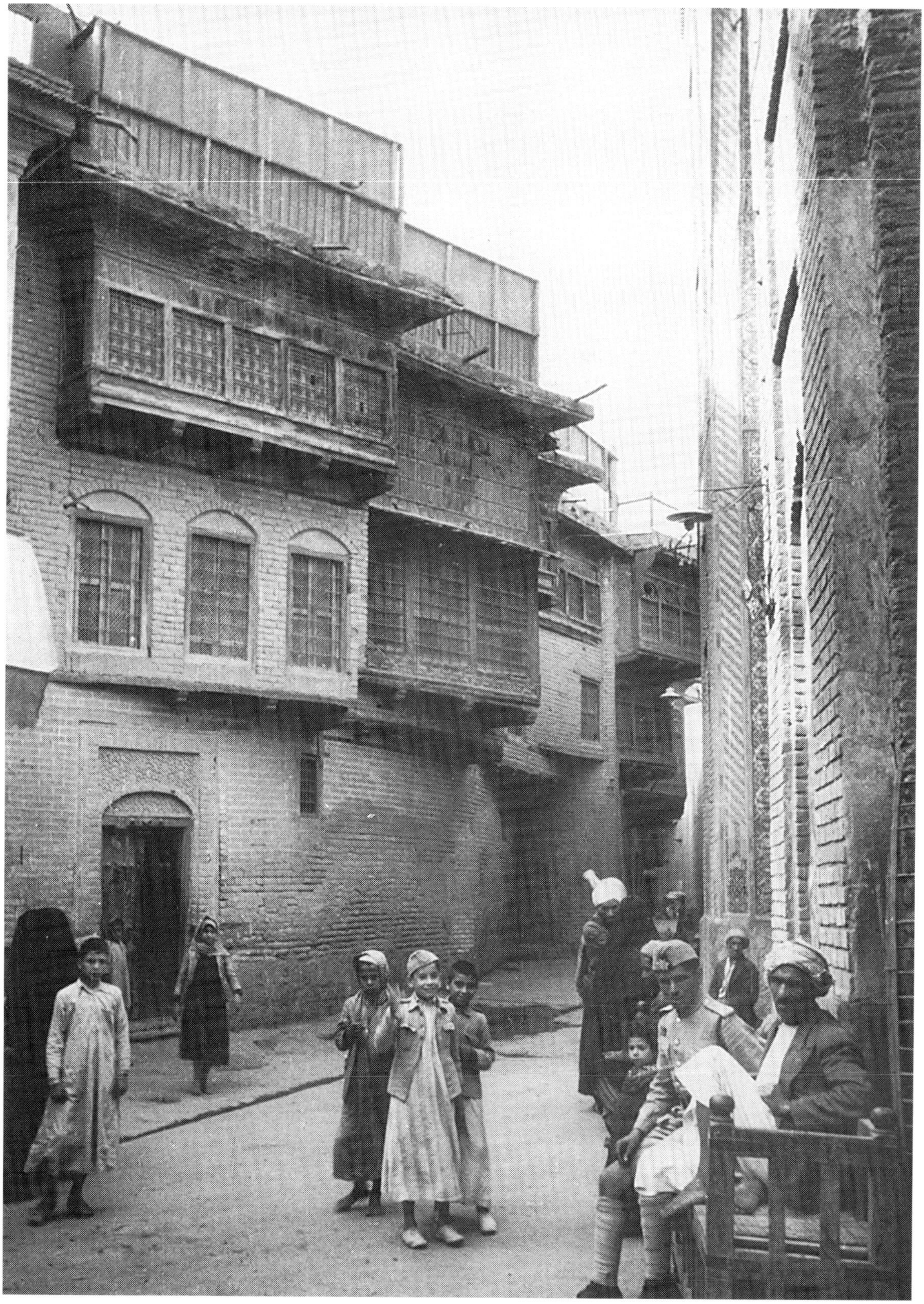

Kadhimain, north of Baghdad 1942

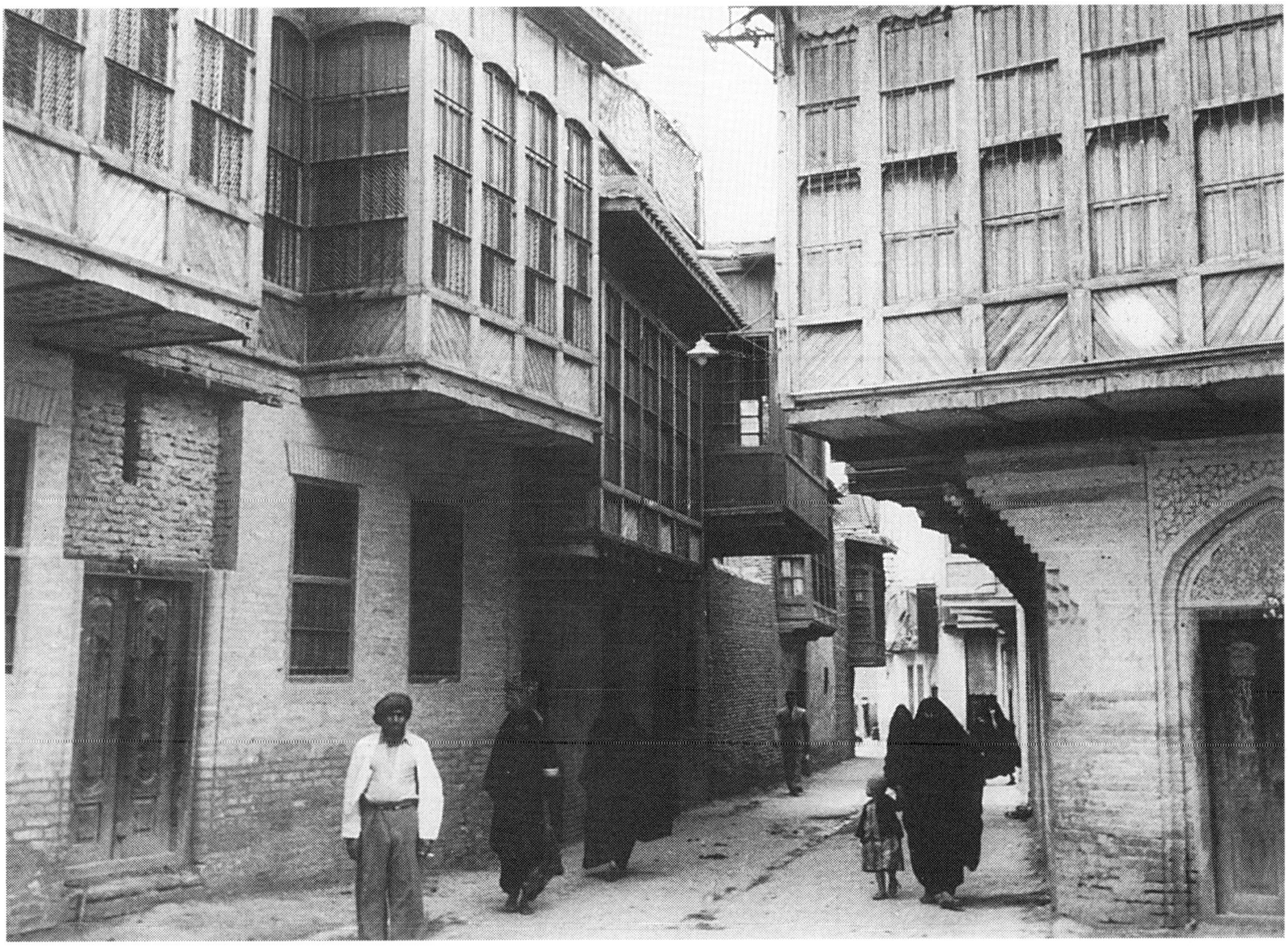

Muadham, near Baghdad 1942

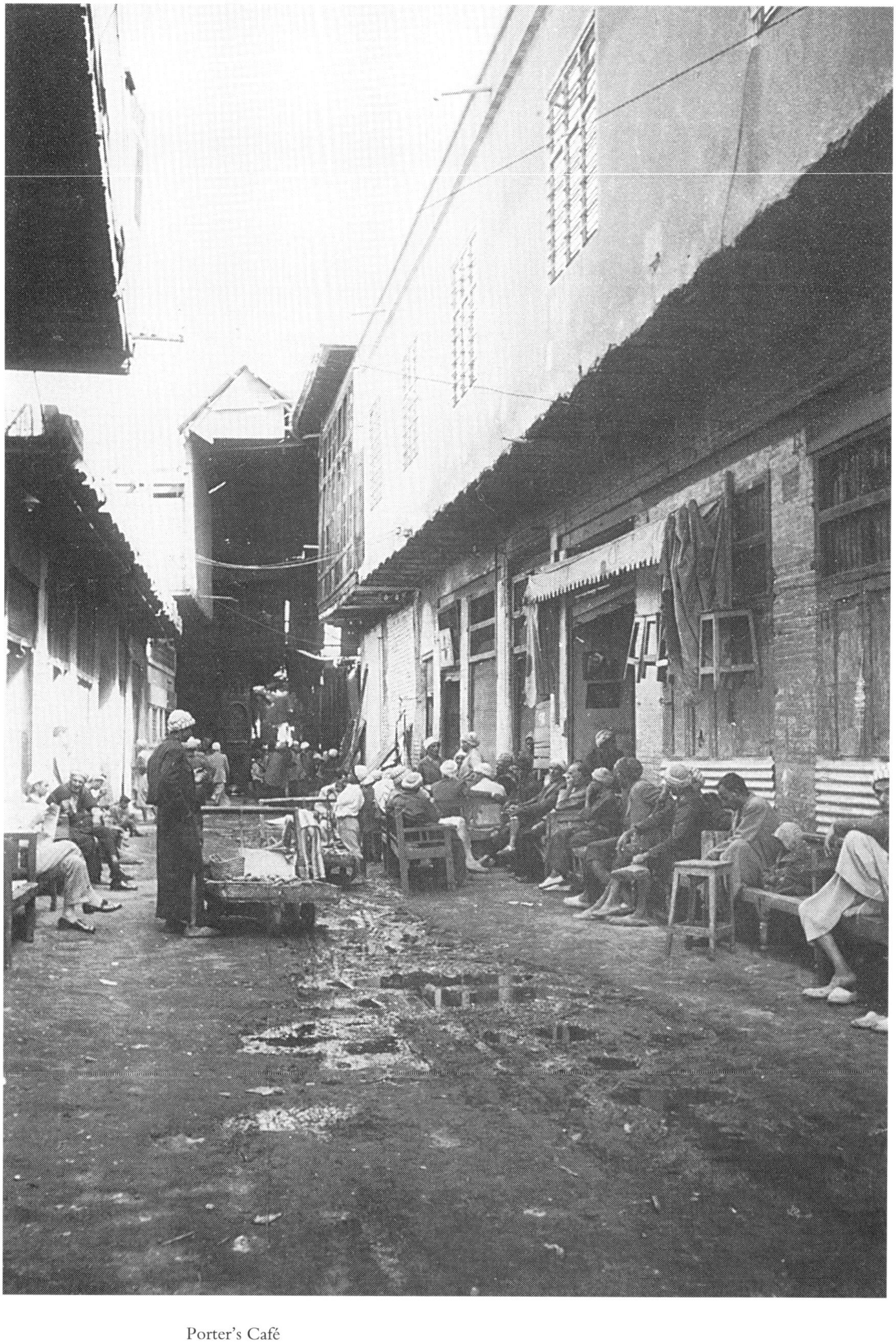

Porter's Café

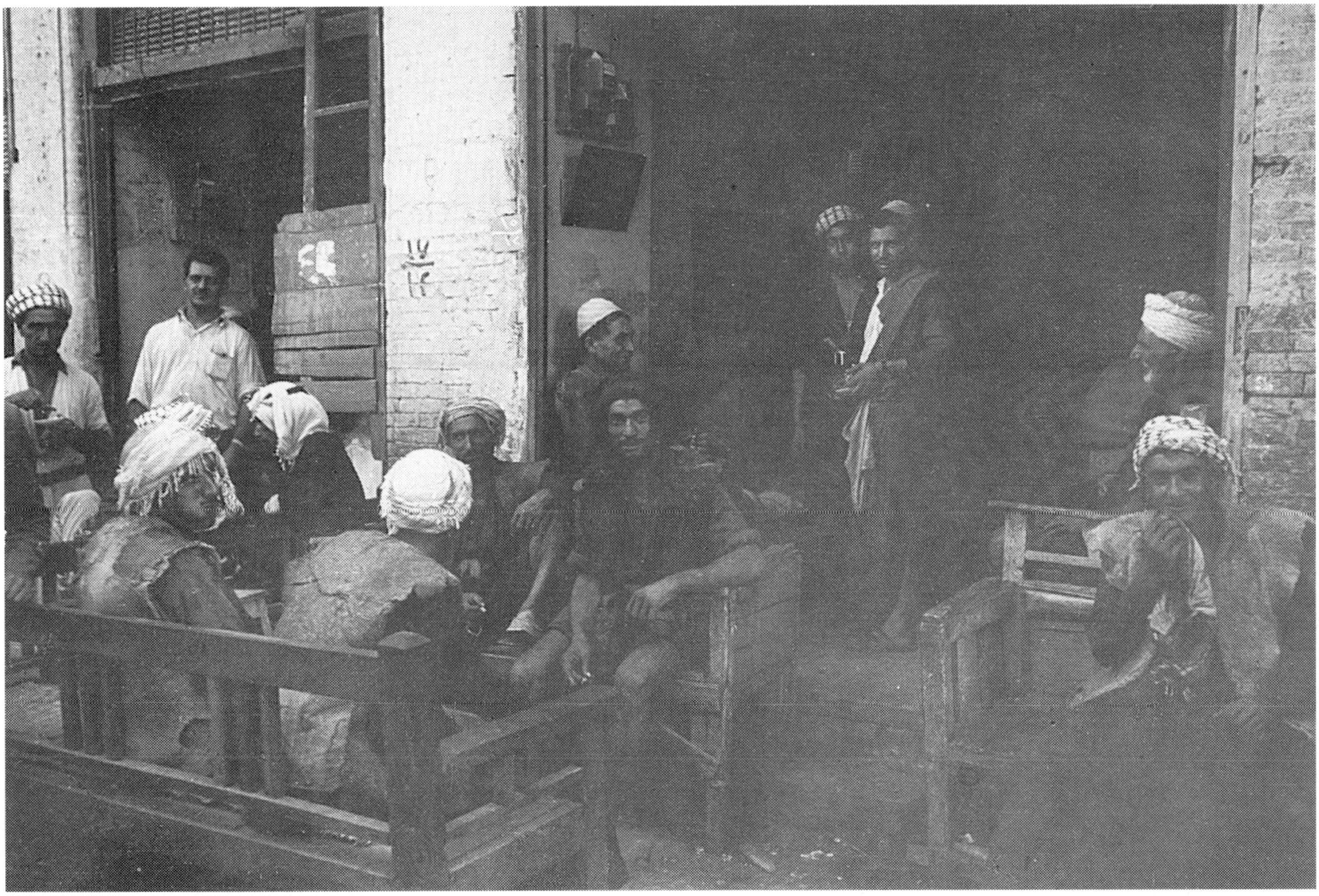

Café of the Lurs

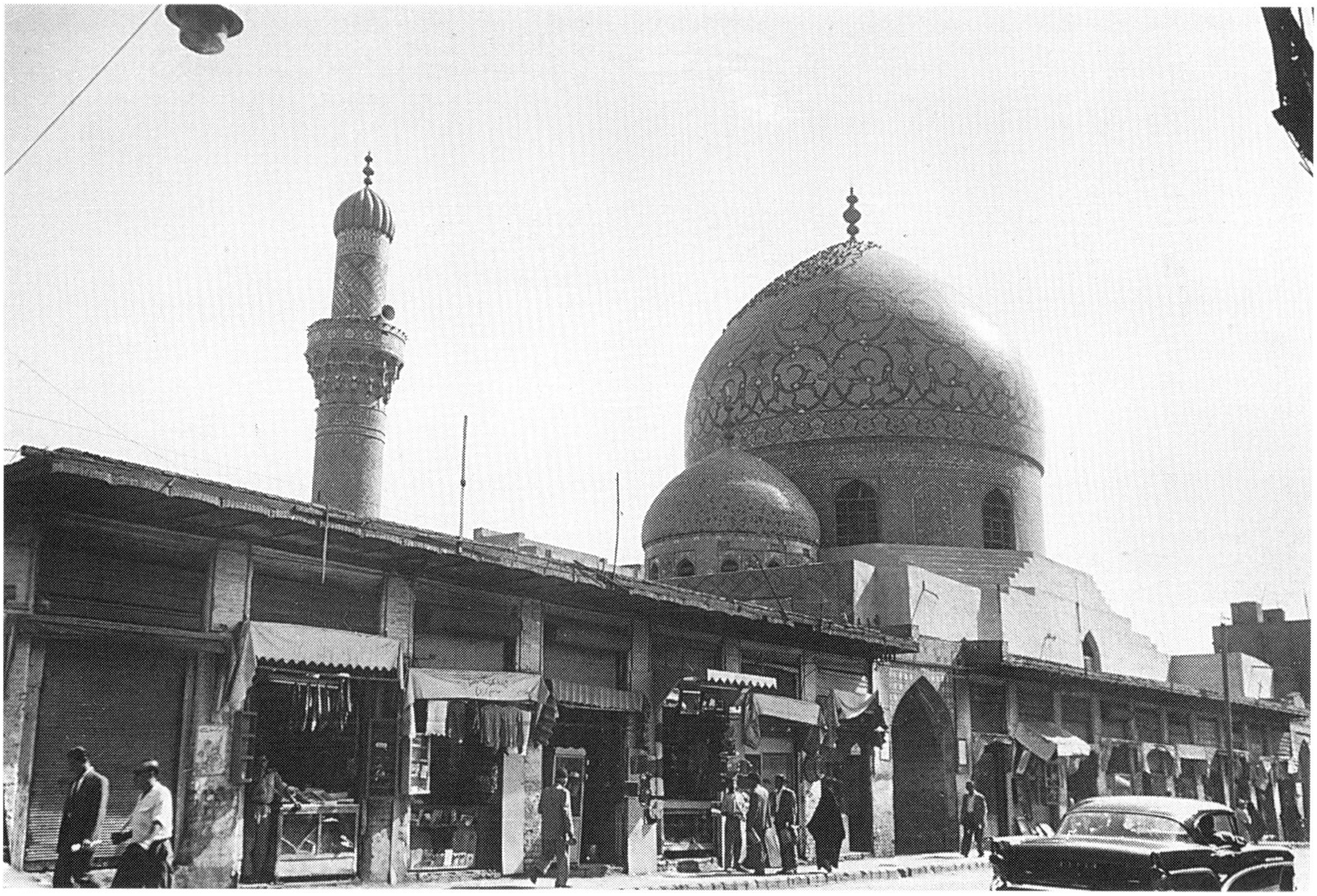

Haidar Khan Mosque 1957

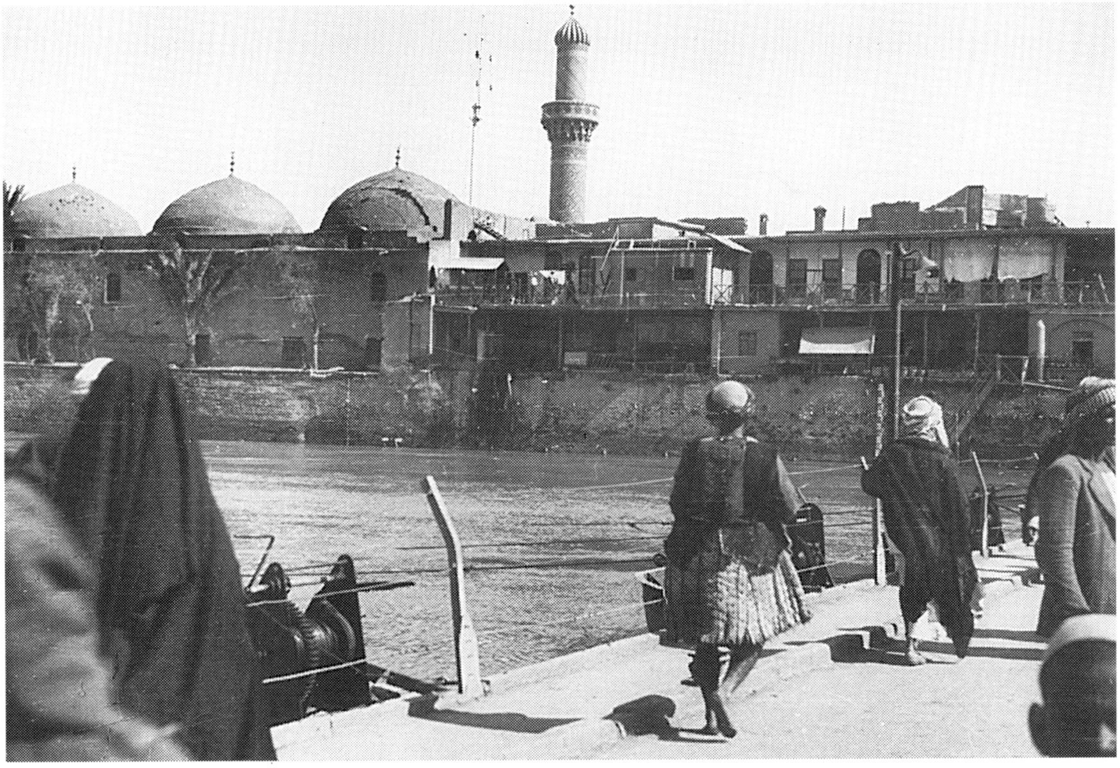

Khota Bridge, West Bank 1933

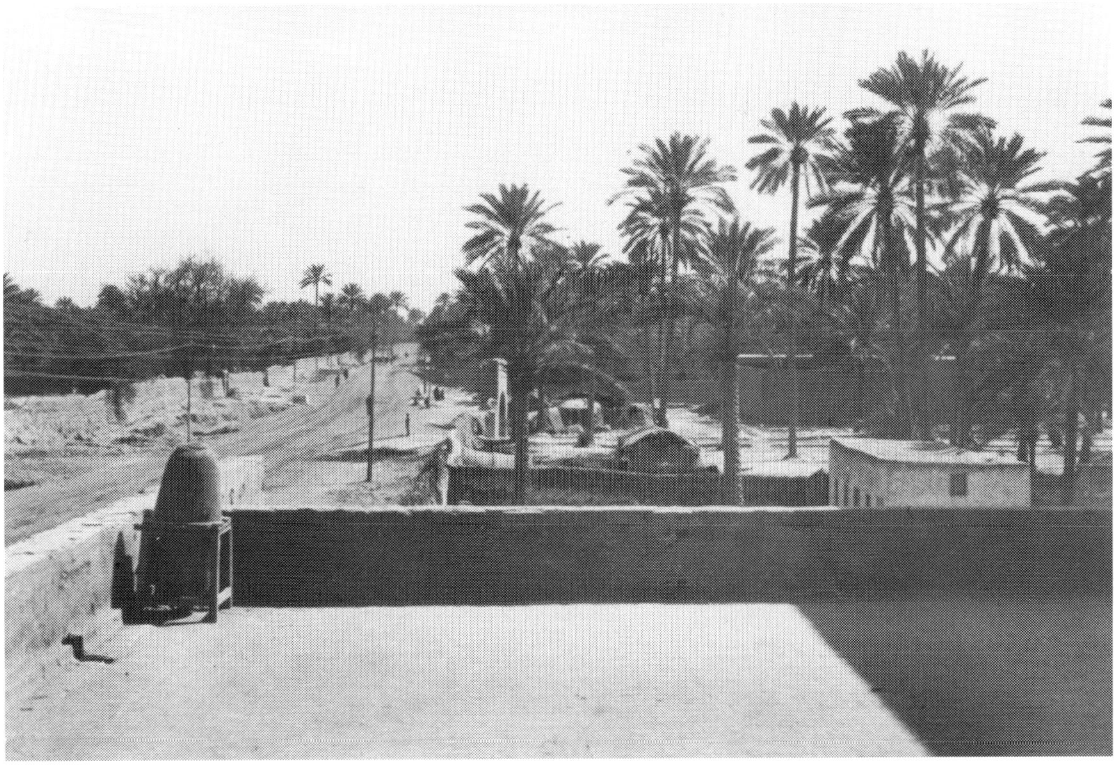

Road to Alawiya from South Gate 1933

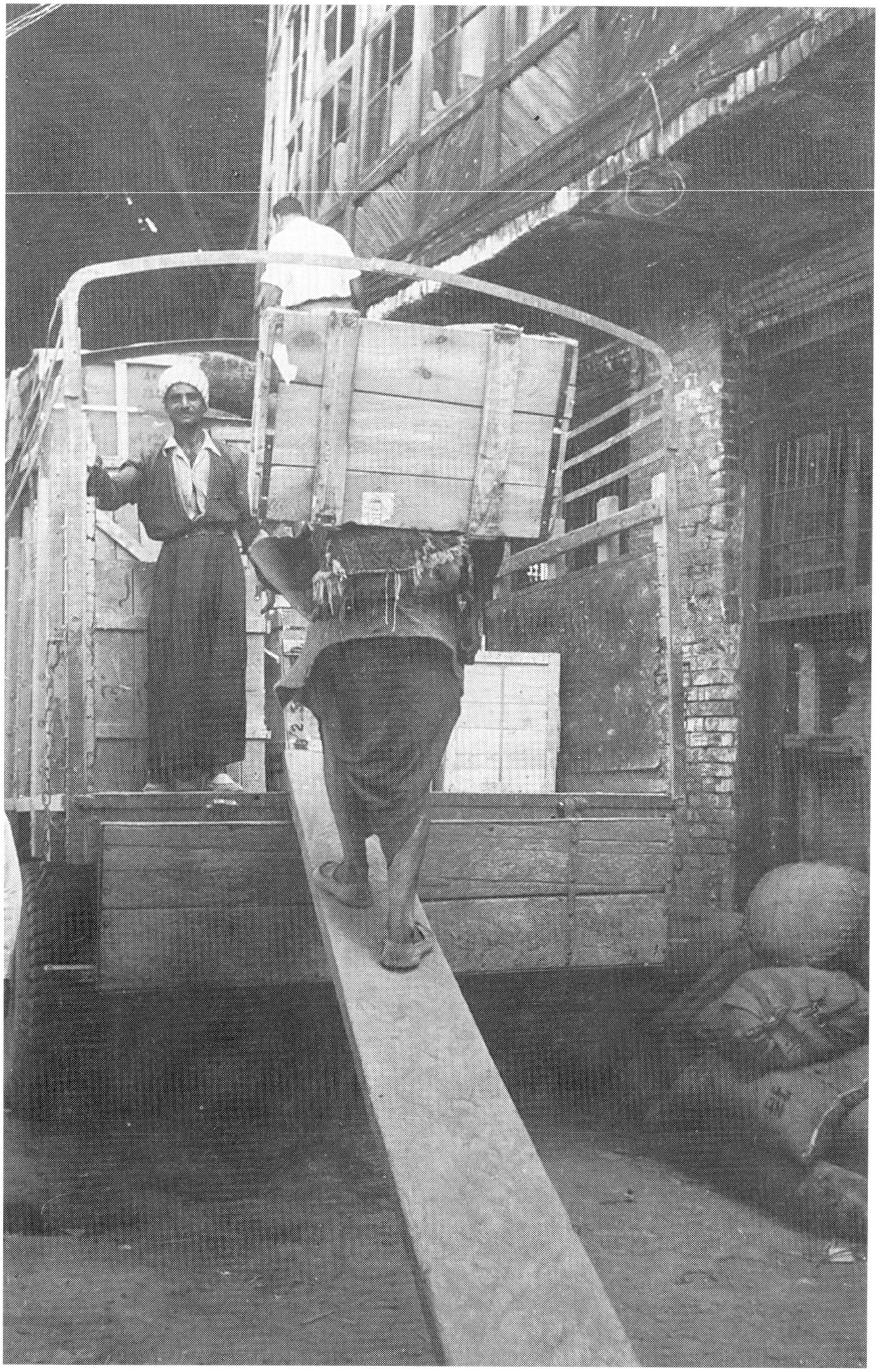

Lur porters 1957

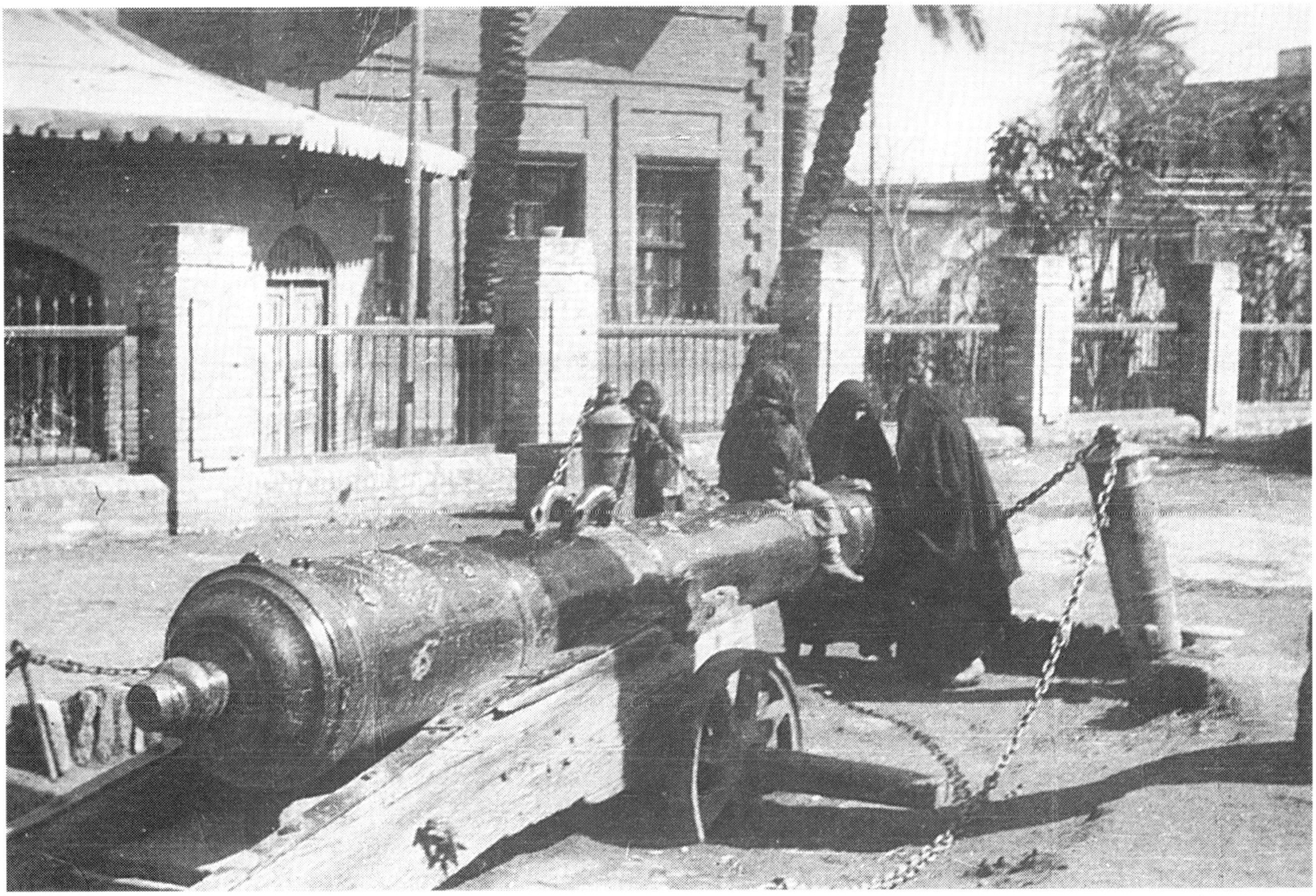

Turkish gun by Serail 1932

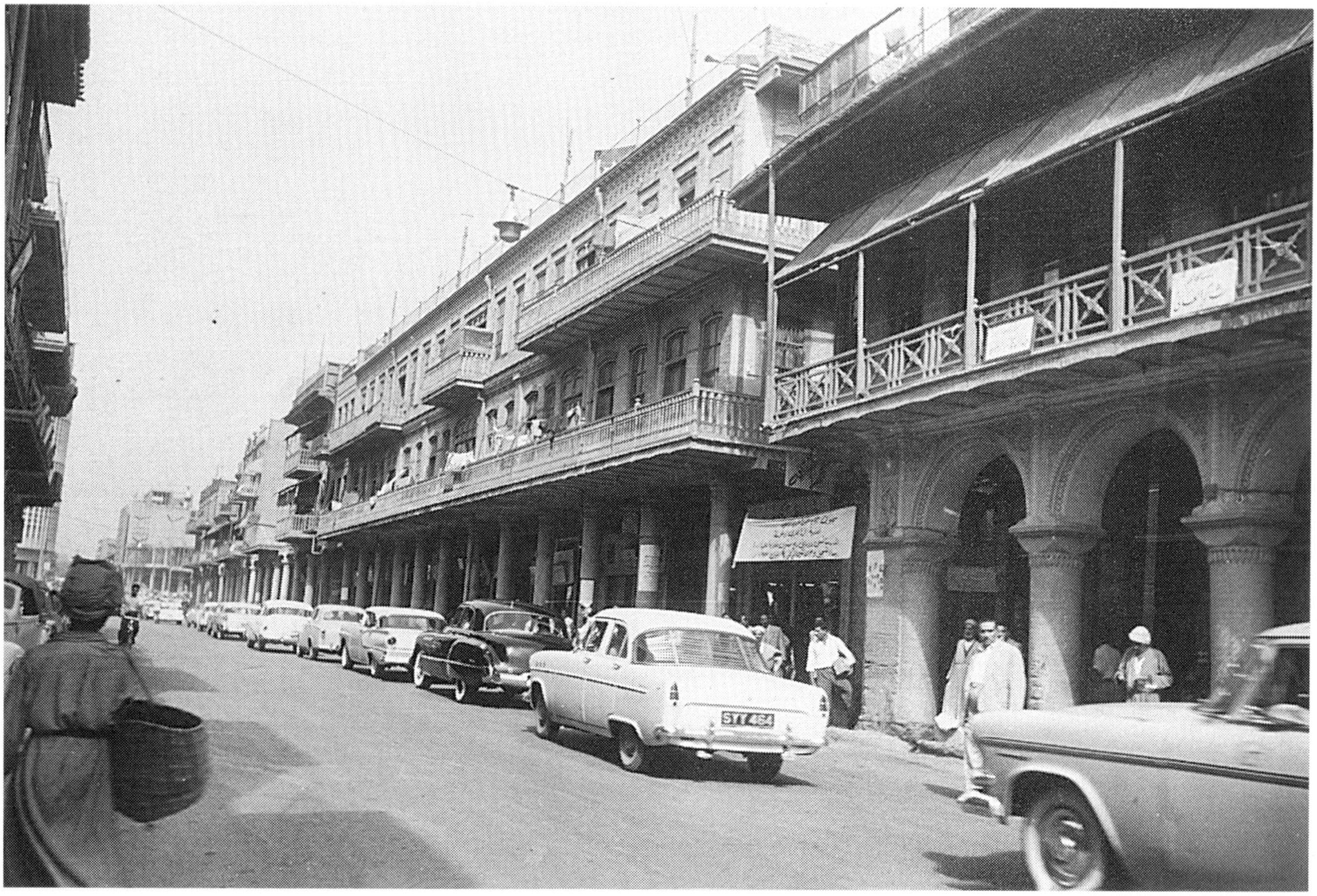

Rashid Street 1957

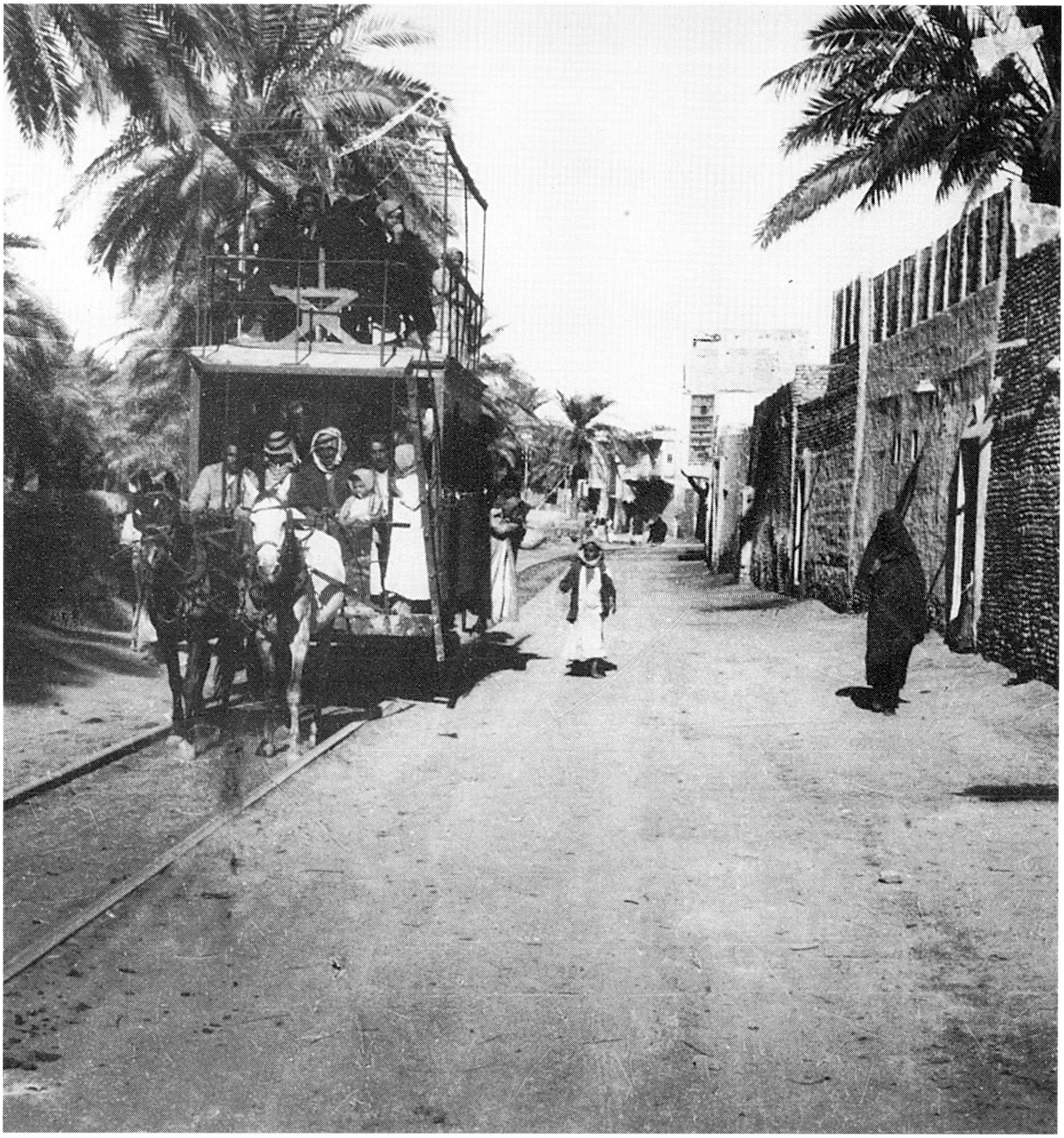

Kadhimain circa 1930. The horse-drawn trams were installed under the modernising regime of Midhat Pasha the Ottoman Governor in about 1870.

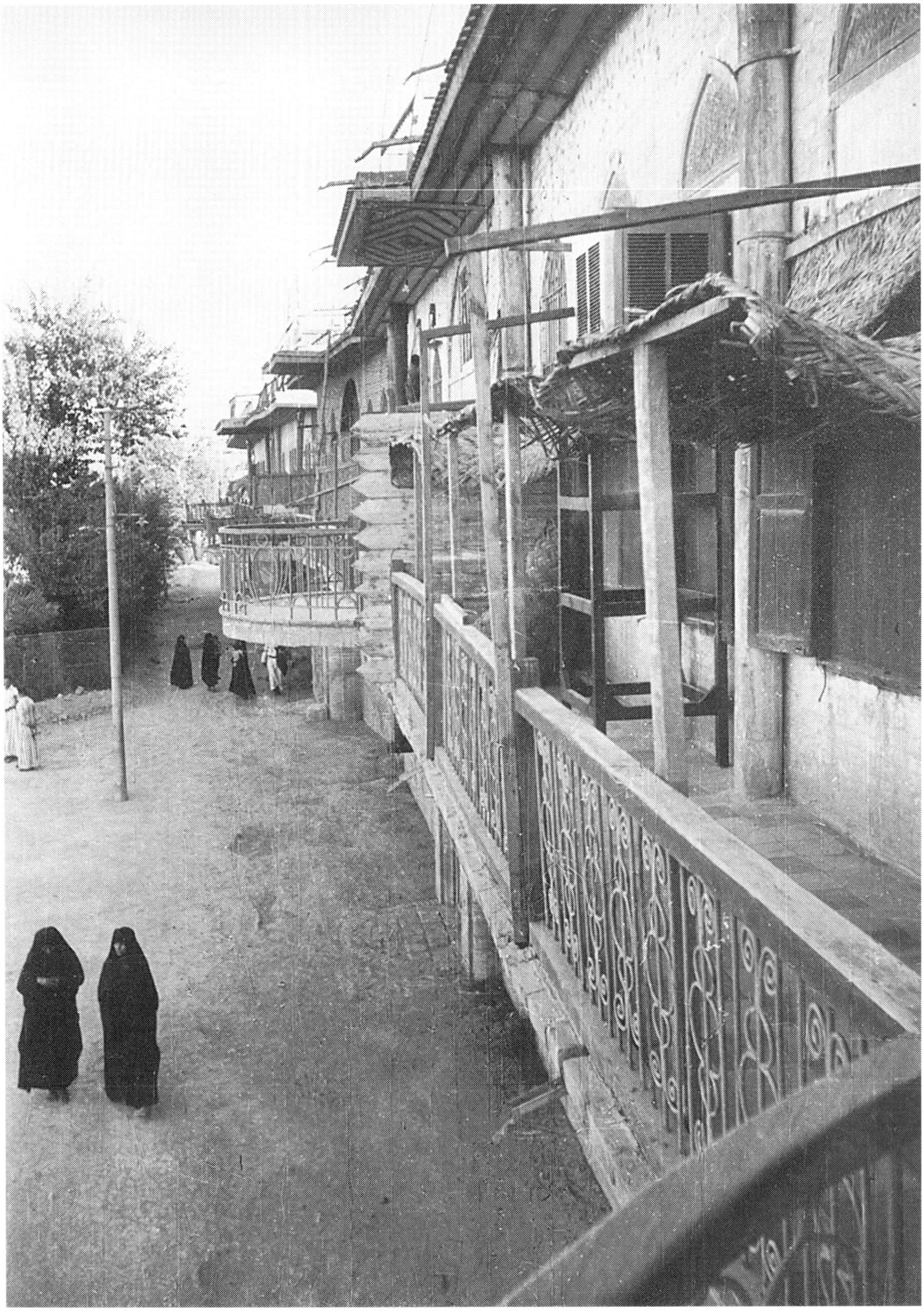

Turkish houses, West Bank 1957

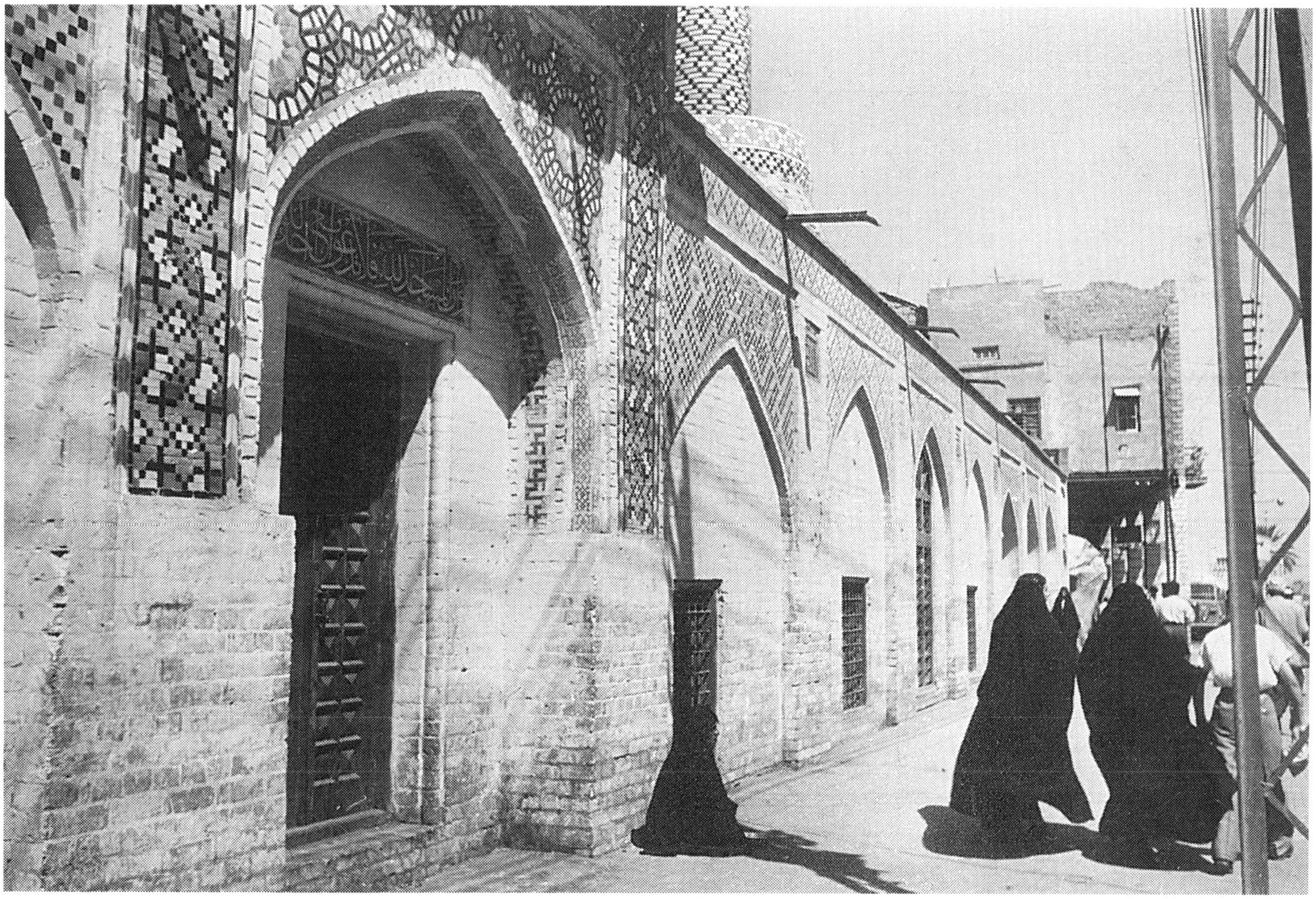

Rashid Street 1954

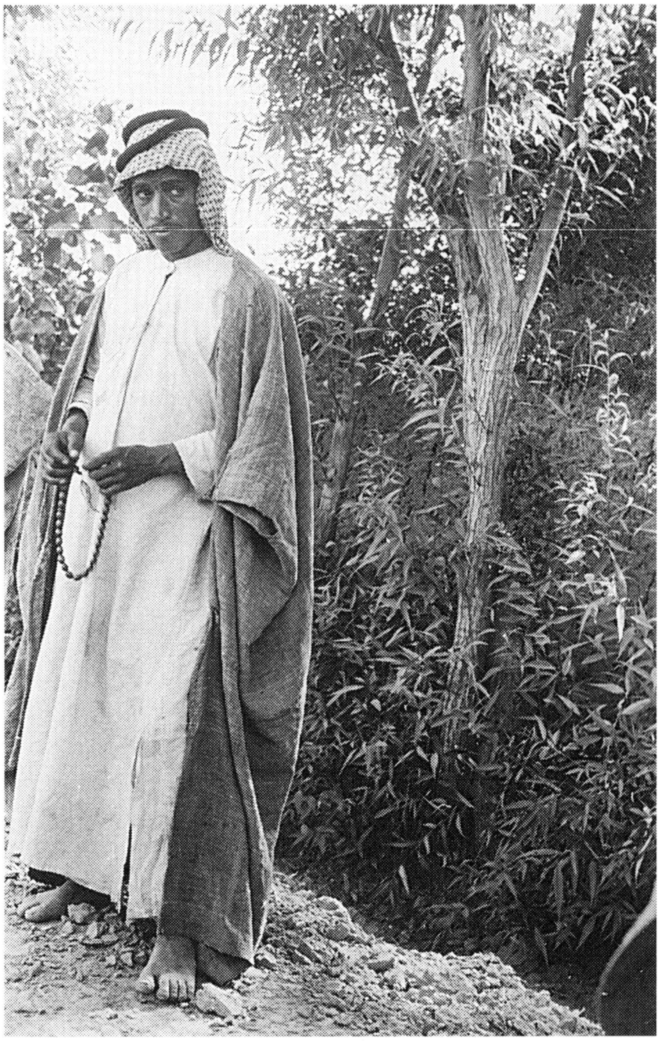

Shia gardener 1937.
Shias wore black and white keffiyehs;
Sunnis wore red and white ones

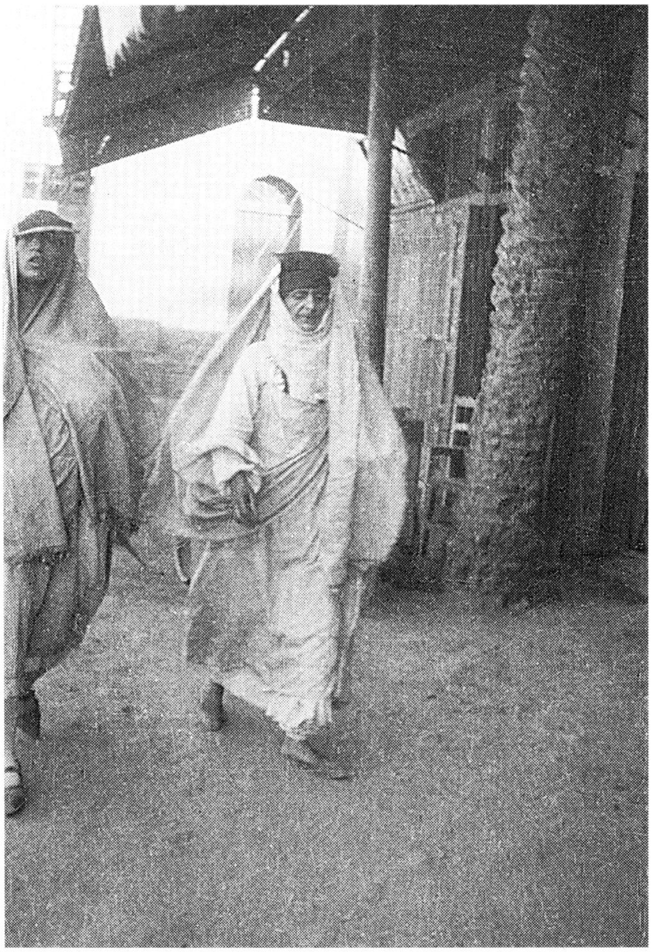

Jewish women 1933

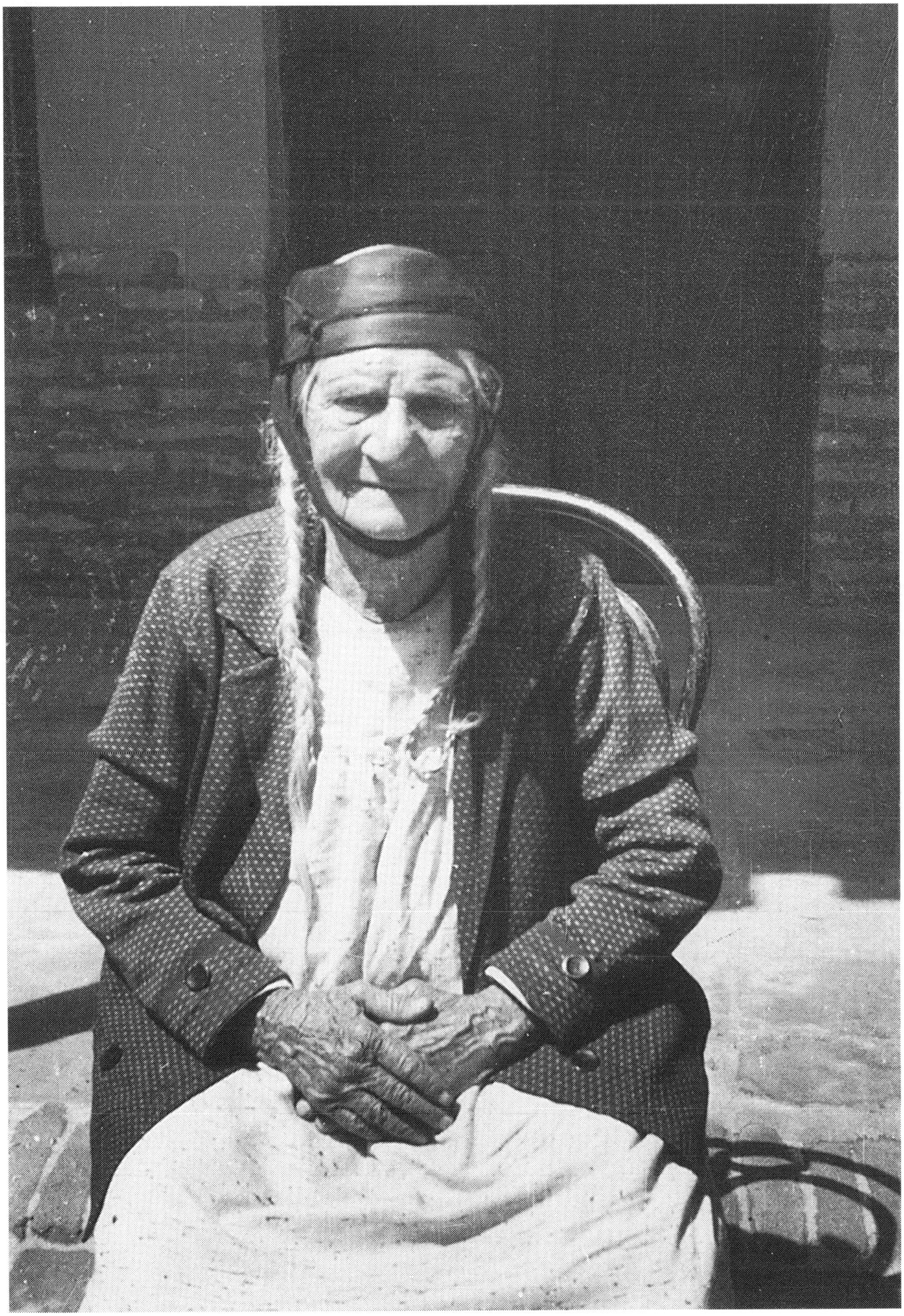

Jacobite Christian woman 1937

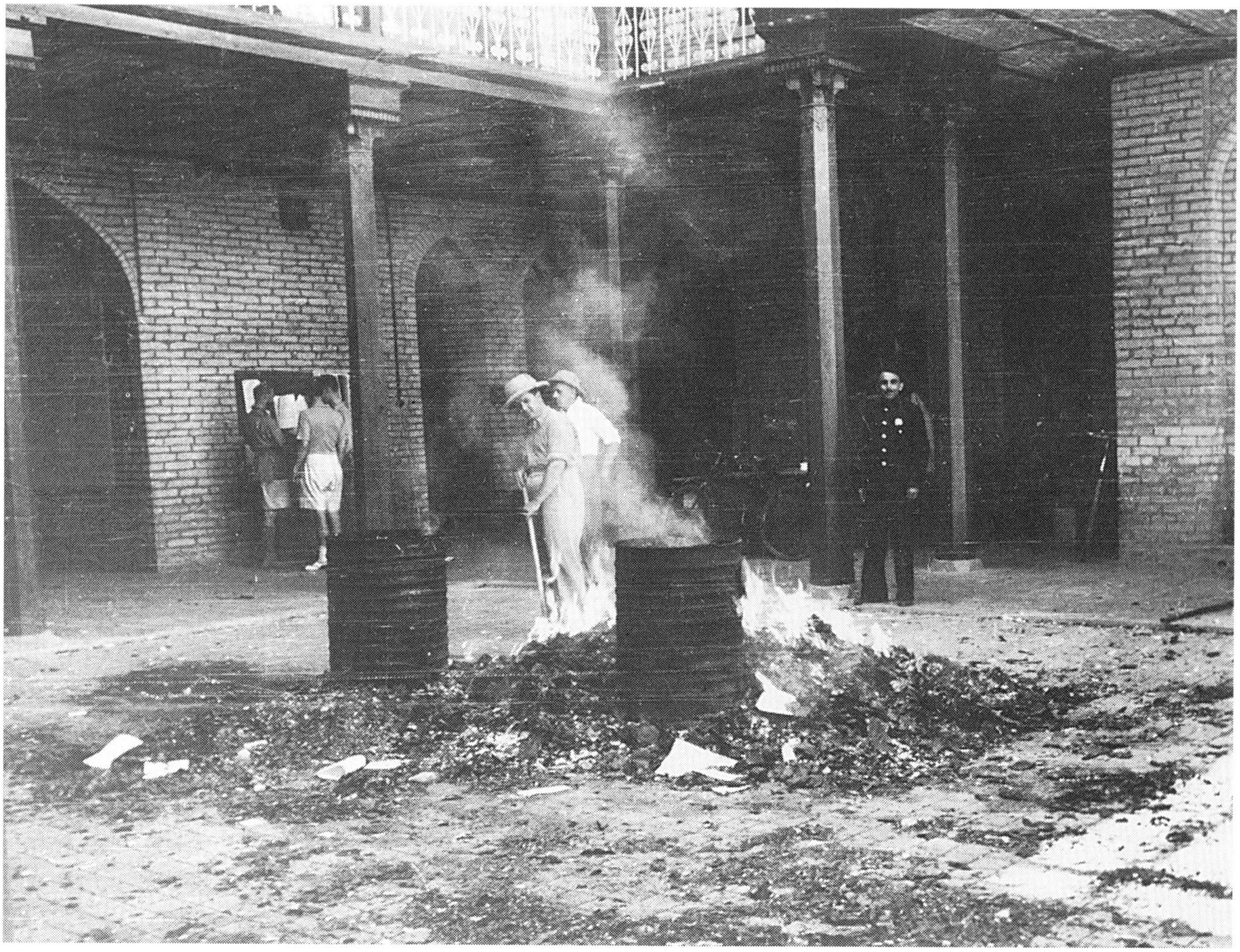

Burning documents in the yard of the British Embassy during the siege, May 1941

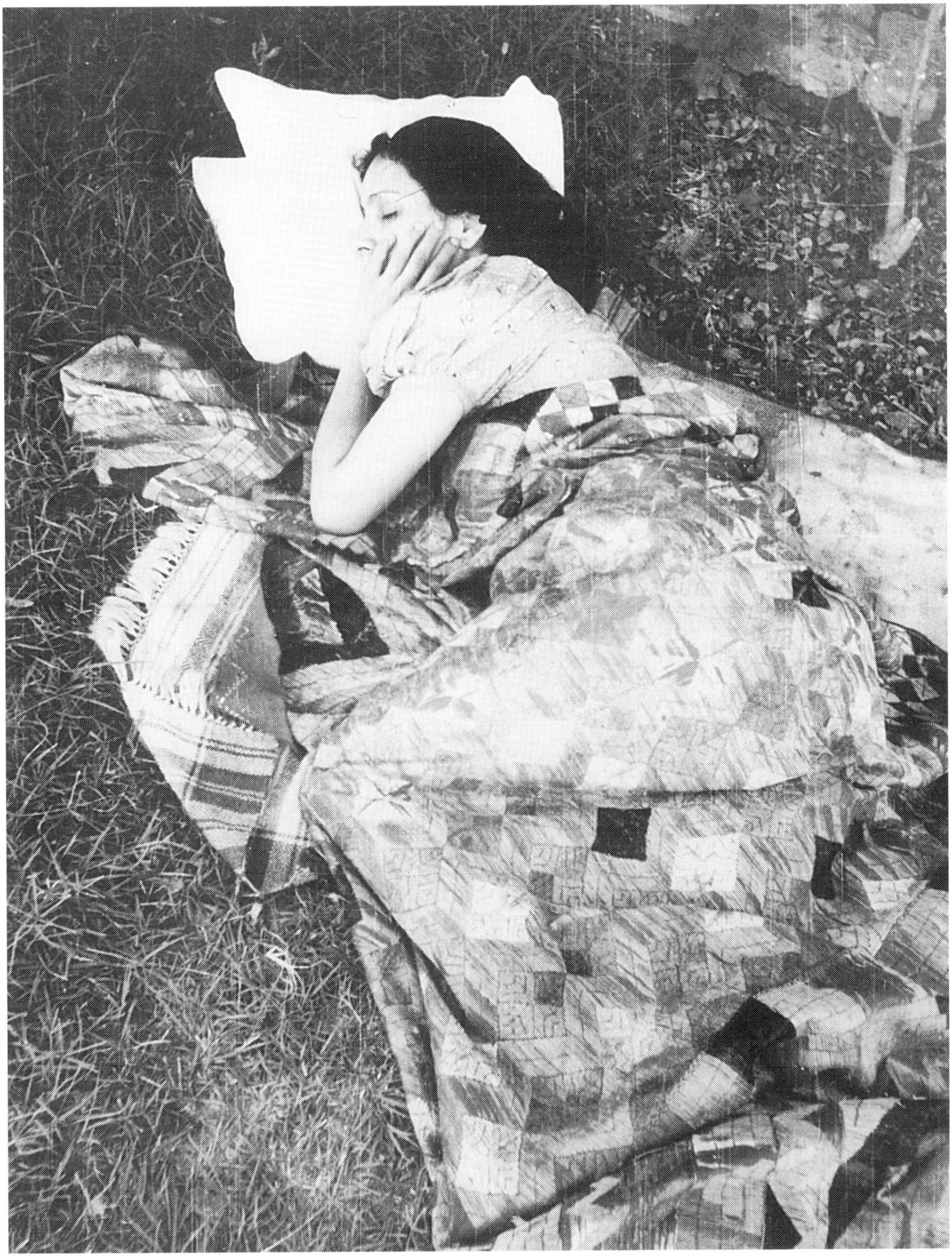

A Jewish refugee in the Embassy garden, May 1941

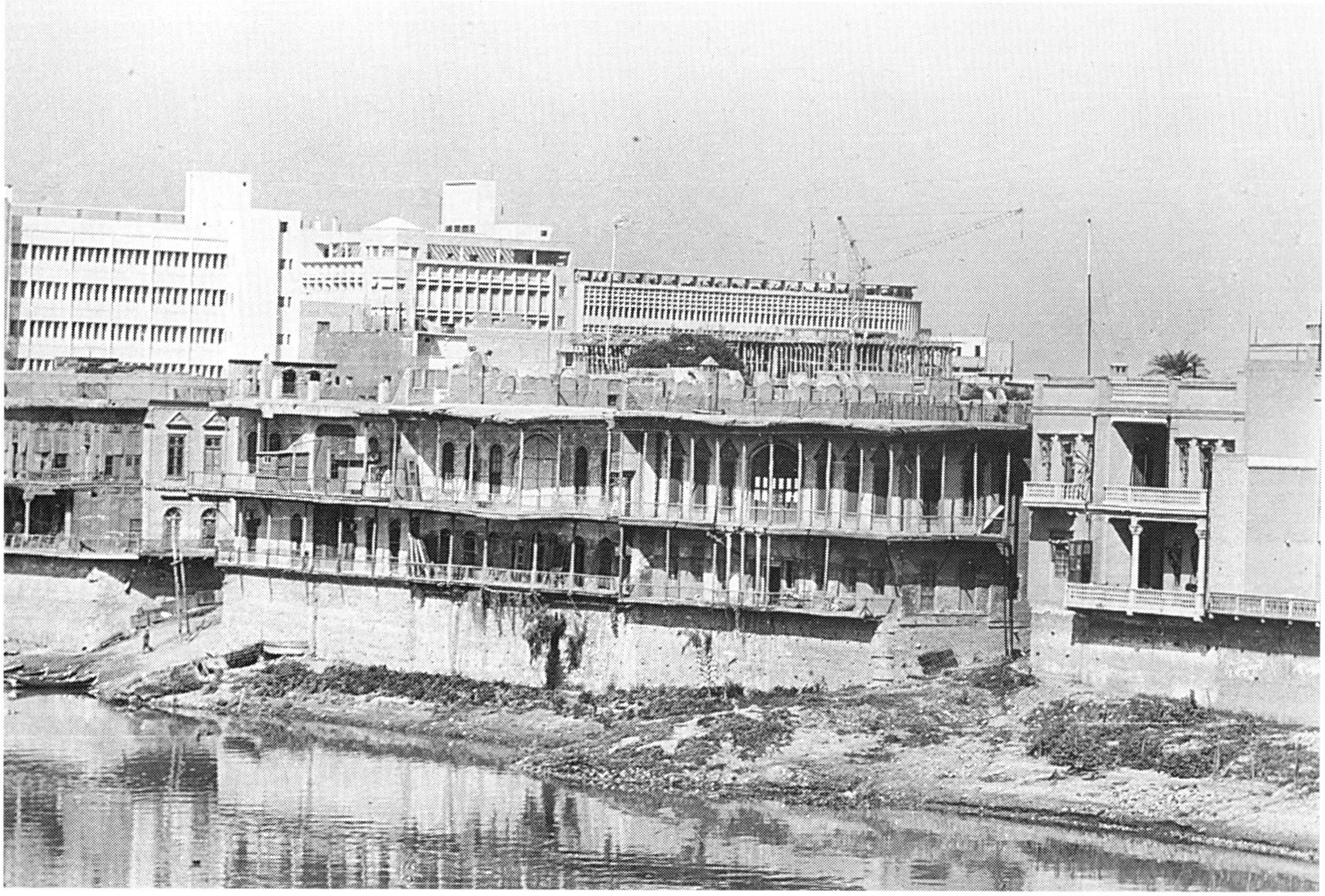

"Modern Baghdad": East Bank 1957

CENTRAL AND SOUTHERN IRAQ

Although she went to considerable lengths to emphasize the distinction between real travellers, who ventured beyond the horizon, and mere tourists who stuck to the beaten track, Freya was a passionate sightseer. On day-trips from Baghdad she would visit ancient sights or beauty spots with diplomatic friends. It was her good fortune to have visited these places before they became generally accessible to tourists, whether local or foreign. She first saw the Arch of Ctesiphon, Iraq's most famous Sassanid monument, on a cold, clear winter's day in 1929, with the mist rising from the yellow earth, creating a mysterious glow which made the arch seem bigger and more lovely as she approached it, until she came "close enough to see it in all its majestic desolation". By 1957, when she visited it again, it was well on the tourist route, with a retaining wall to protect the crumbling bricks and the inevitable urchin selling tepid Coca-Cola: at the back of her photograph Freya pencilled the legend: "For worse or better."

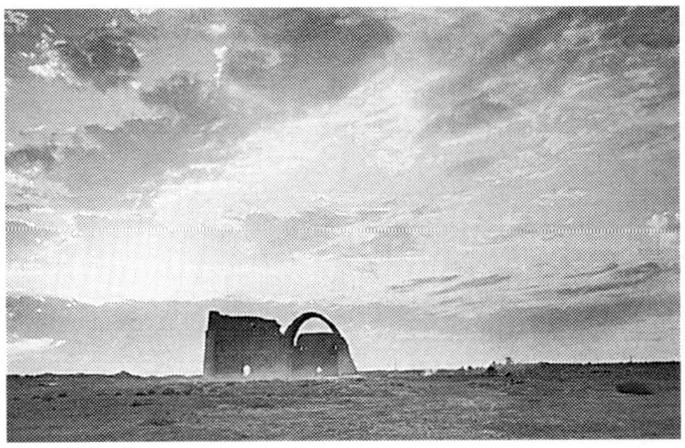

Arch of Ctesiphon
circa 1929

The equally impressive walls of Ukhaidr in the desert, two hours' drive from Baghdad, she saw for the first time in 1937. "There is nothing quite like this finding of ruins in the desert, something so august in its nakedness, and so dignified in man's courage and helplessness against the passing of Time." She was just as moved when she revisited it twenty years later, in October 1957; but returning by way of the Shithatha Oasis, where she had remembered the sulphur springs welling "clear and strangely blue" among the palm trees, she was disappointed. The springs were now surrounded by a wall for hygienic purposes, and the magic had gone. On the same trip she revisited the Shiite shrine of Kerbala, where the Imam Hussein, the Prophet's grandson, is buried and bravely took a picture of the women waiting outside. On her earlier visit twenty years before, such audacity would have been unthinkable.

Most of the places Freya recorded in Iraq have been transformed beyond recognition – by "progress", politics or war. As early as 1930 she observed the fanatical hatred the "young effendis" had for anything old and the fierce contempt they held for antiquity. The most poignant and devastating example of this attitude would be the draining of the marshes north of Basra, where the Tigris and Euphrates meet to form the Shatt al Arab. The project was launched in 1992 by Saddam Hussein, to punish the Marsh Arabs, who are Shiites, for allegedly supporting a rebellion against his government by Shiites in Basra.

The Marshes, supposedly the site of the Garden of Eden, sustained a way of life extending back to Sumerian times. The beautifully crafted reed-houses made and re-made by the people of the marshes were among the oldest continuously inhabited human structures in the world. Freya visited them in May 1943, as part of her work for the Brotherhood. She spent a day with one of the Sheikhs who had grown rich from the rice grown on land reclaimed from the rivers. With the wealth of their rice, the chiefs were beginning to build stone houses in the pasture lands above the flood line; but they kept their beautiful reed halls for guests, where the light filtered through vaulted sheaves and plaited mats, creating a cathedral-like atmosphere. Gliding through the still waters, she experienced the enchantment of this Eden before the Fall, where sunlight flickered with myriad shadows through the reeds, where the kingfishers dived and flies gently buzzed in the sun. The charm of the Marshes, she concluded, oblivious to the malignant possibilities of bulldozers allied to military power, "is loneliness, the opening of a door, the sharing of a secret with a world that is as it was and will be, before and after the visitings of men".

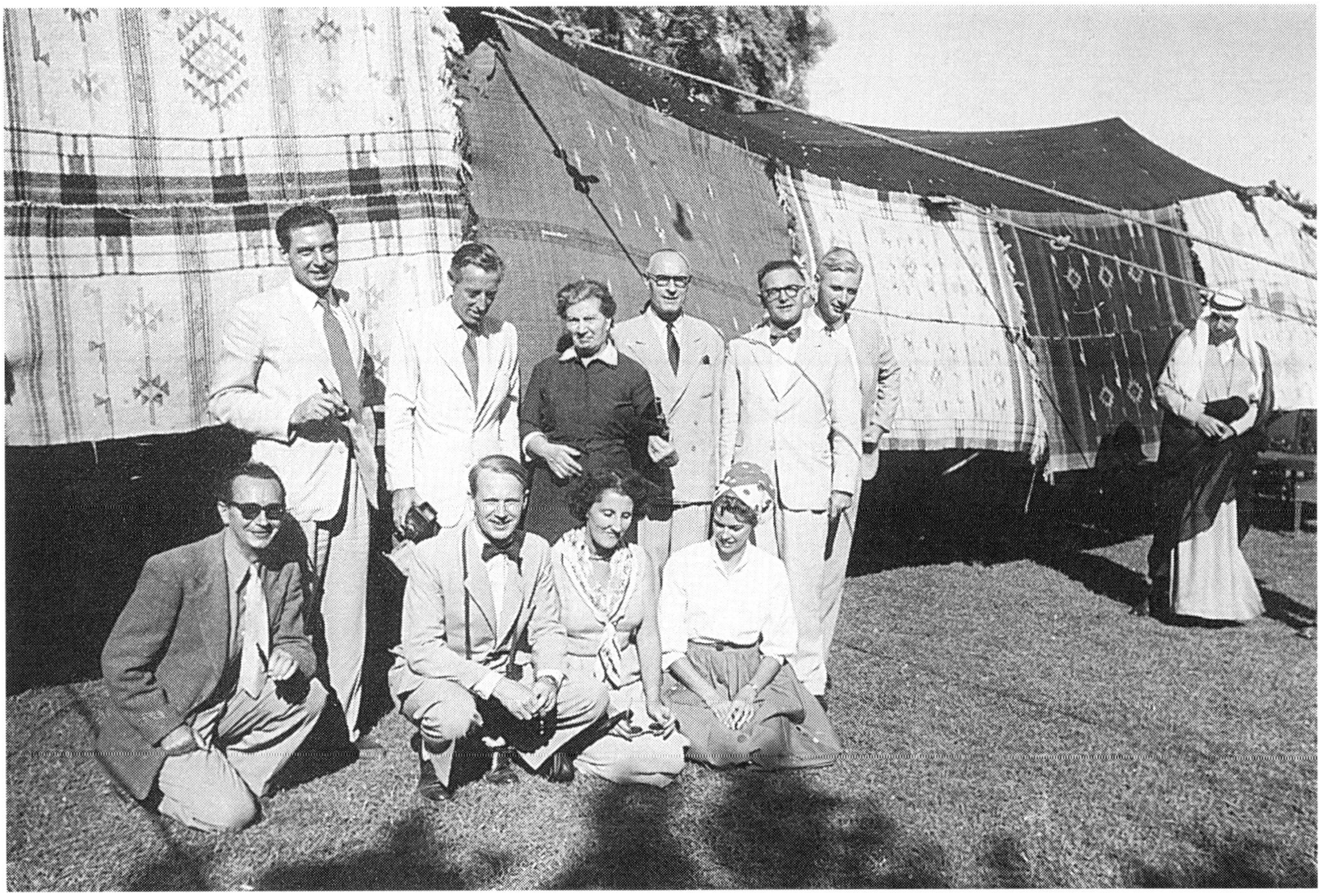

A diplomatic outing circa 1940.

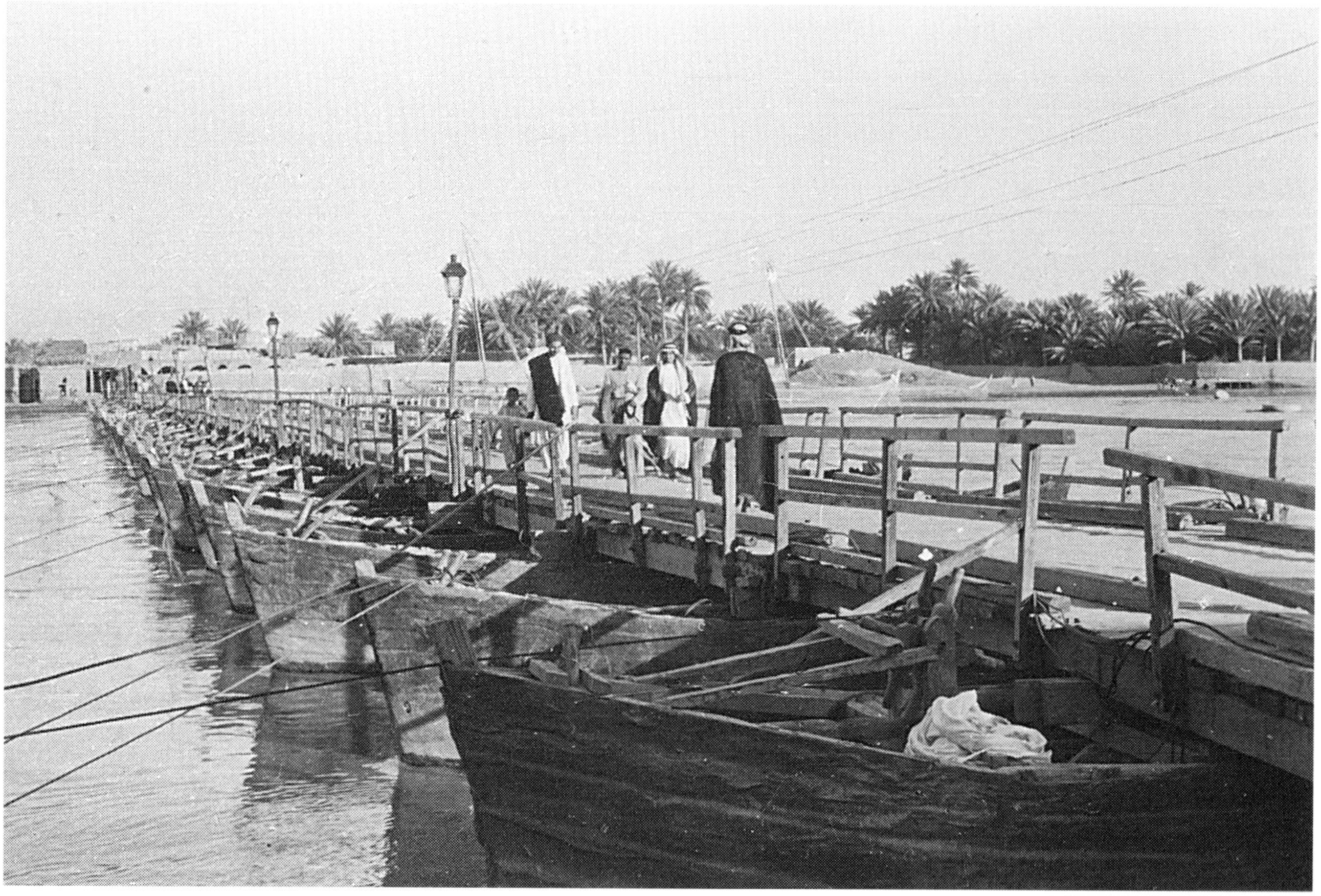

Pontoon Bridge over the Tigris near Al Hillah 1937

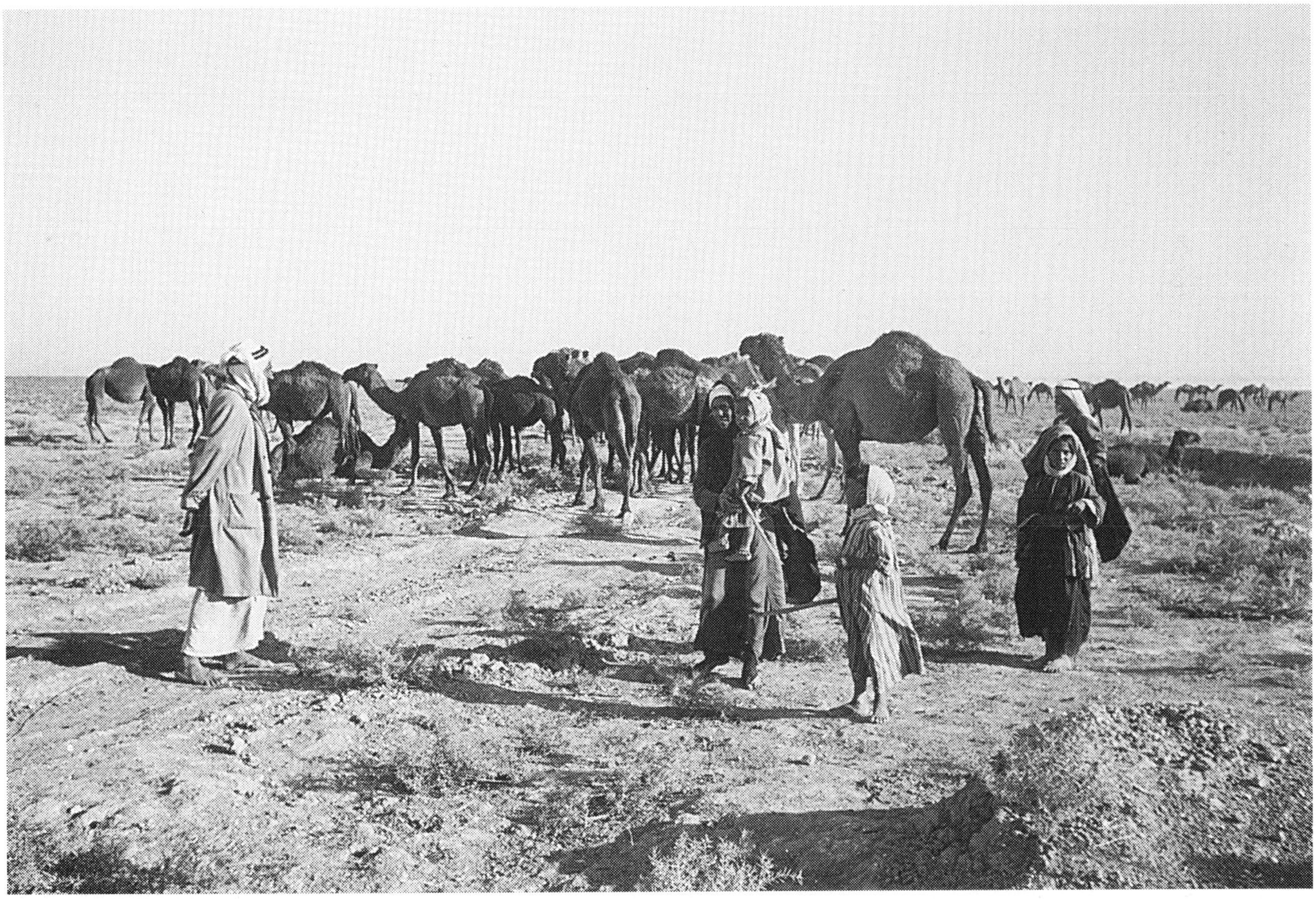

West of Baghdad 1957

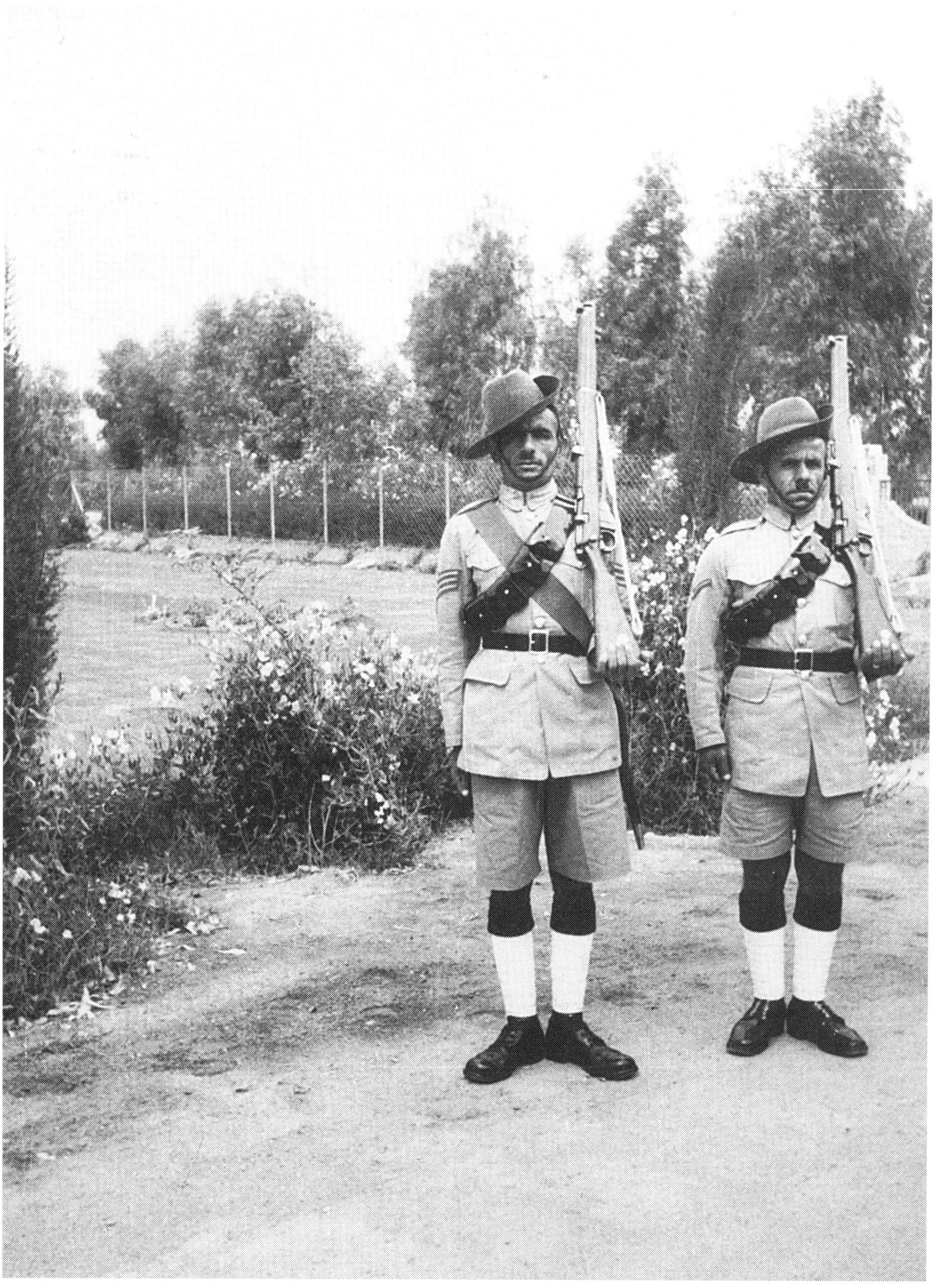

Assyrian levies at Habbaniyah base 1941

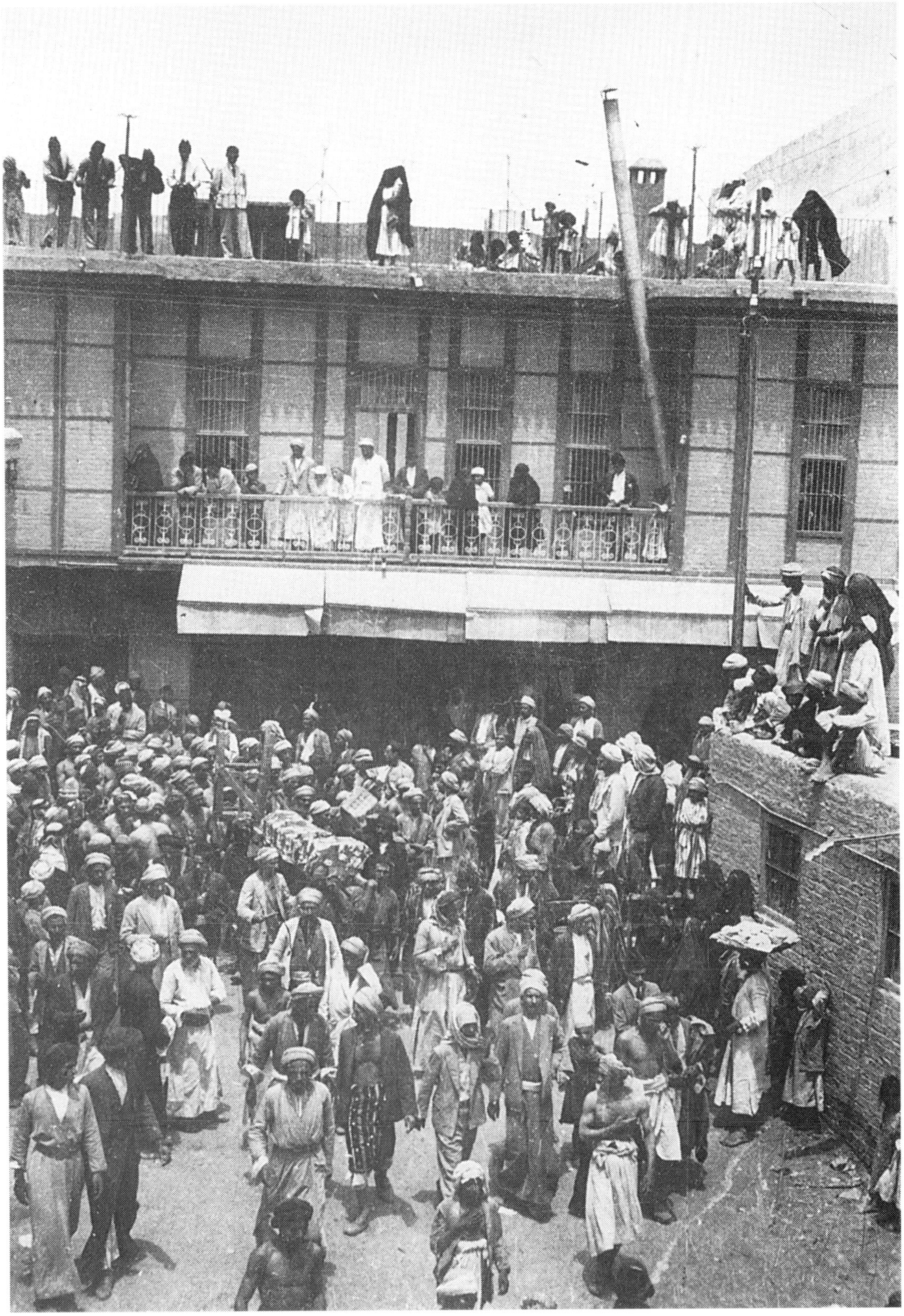

Muharram festivities 1941

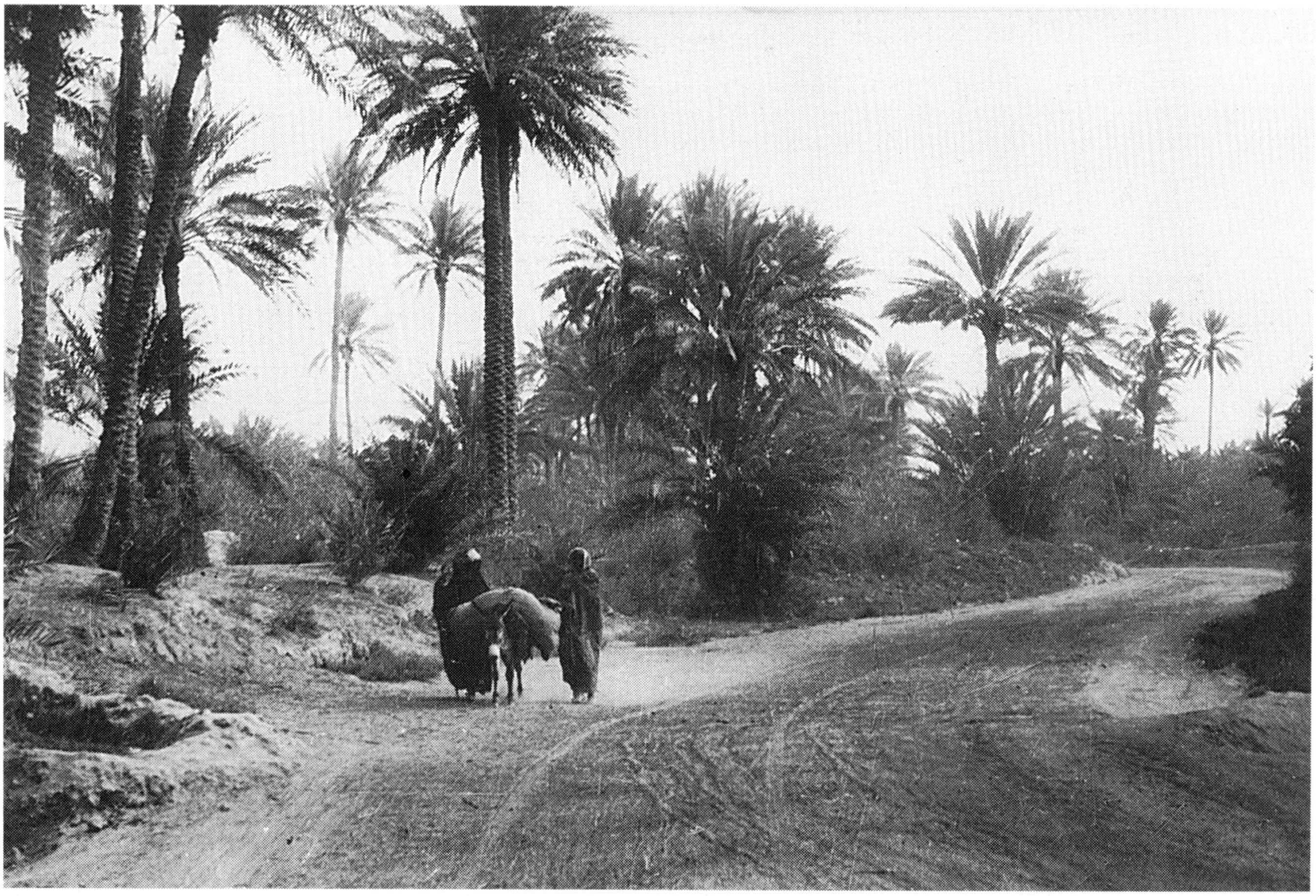

Kerbala Gardens 1942

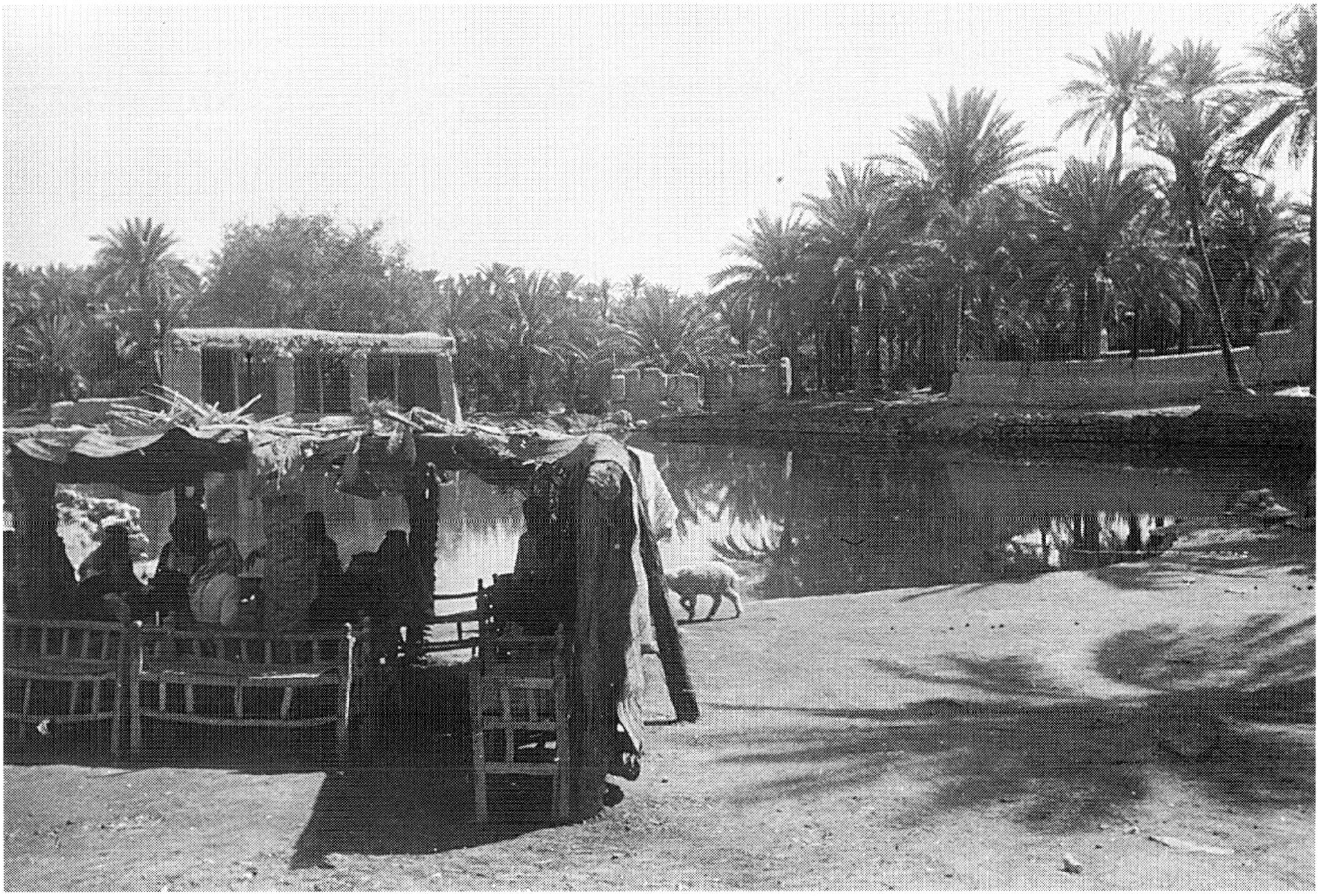

Shithatha 1937

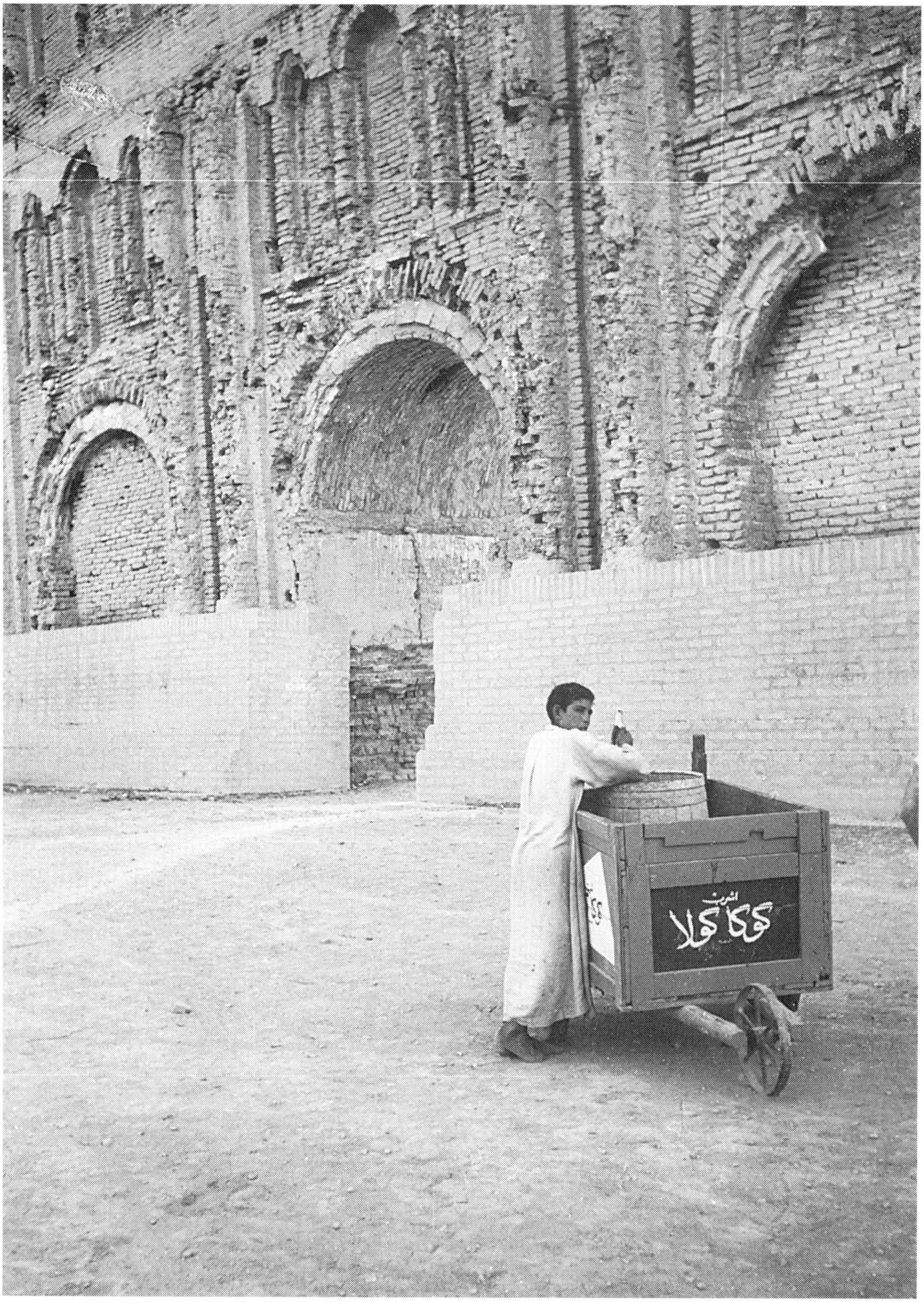

Coca-Cola seller Arch of Ctesiphon 1957

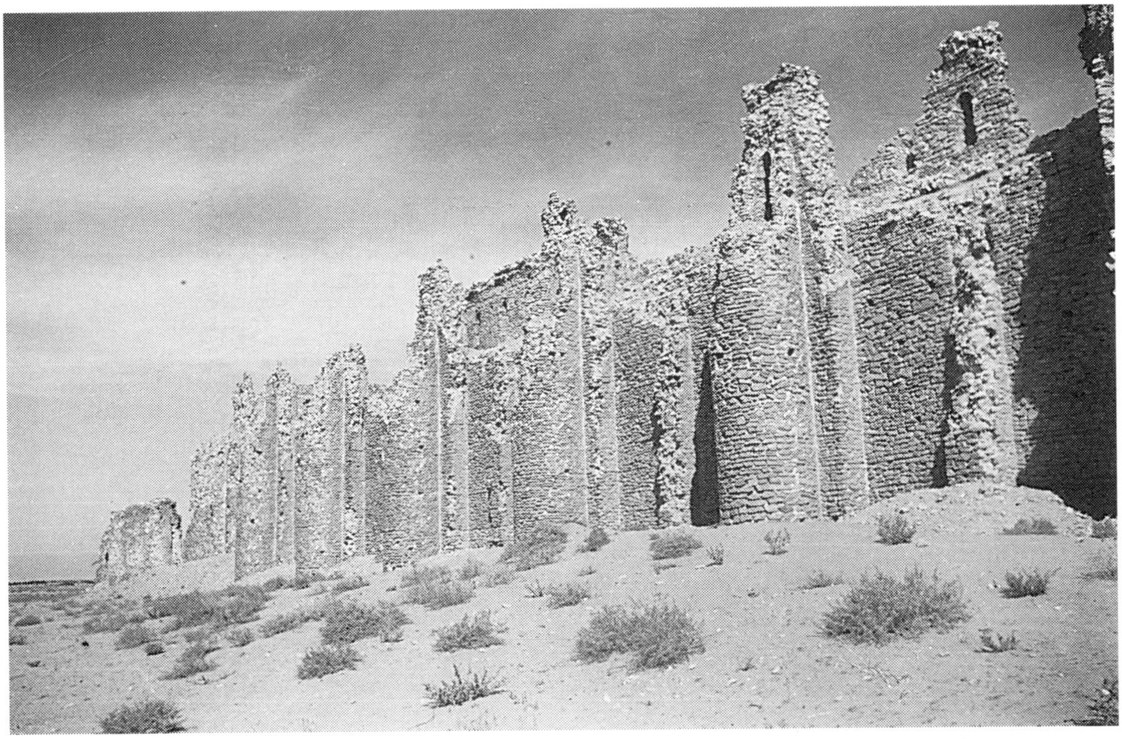

Ukhaidr 1957

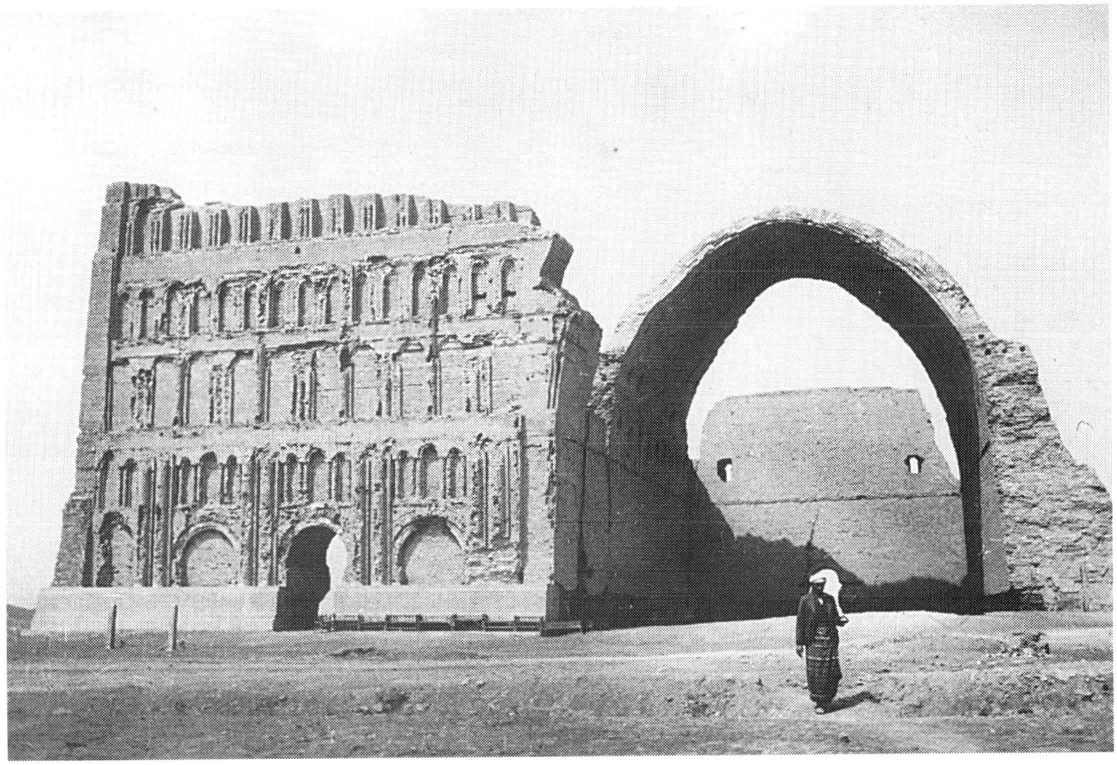

Arch of Ctesiphon 1941

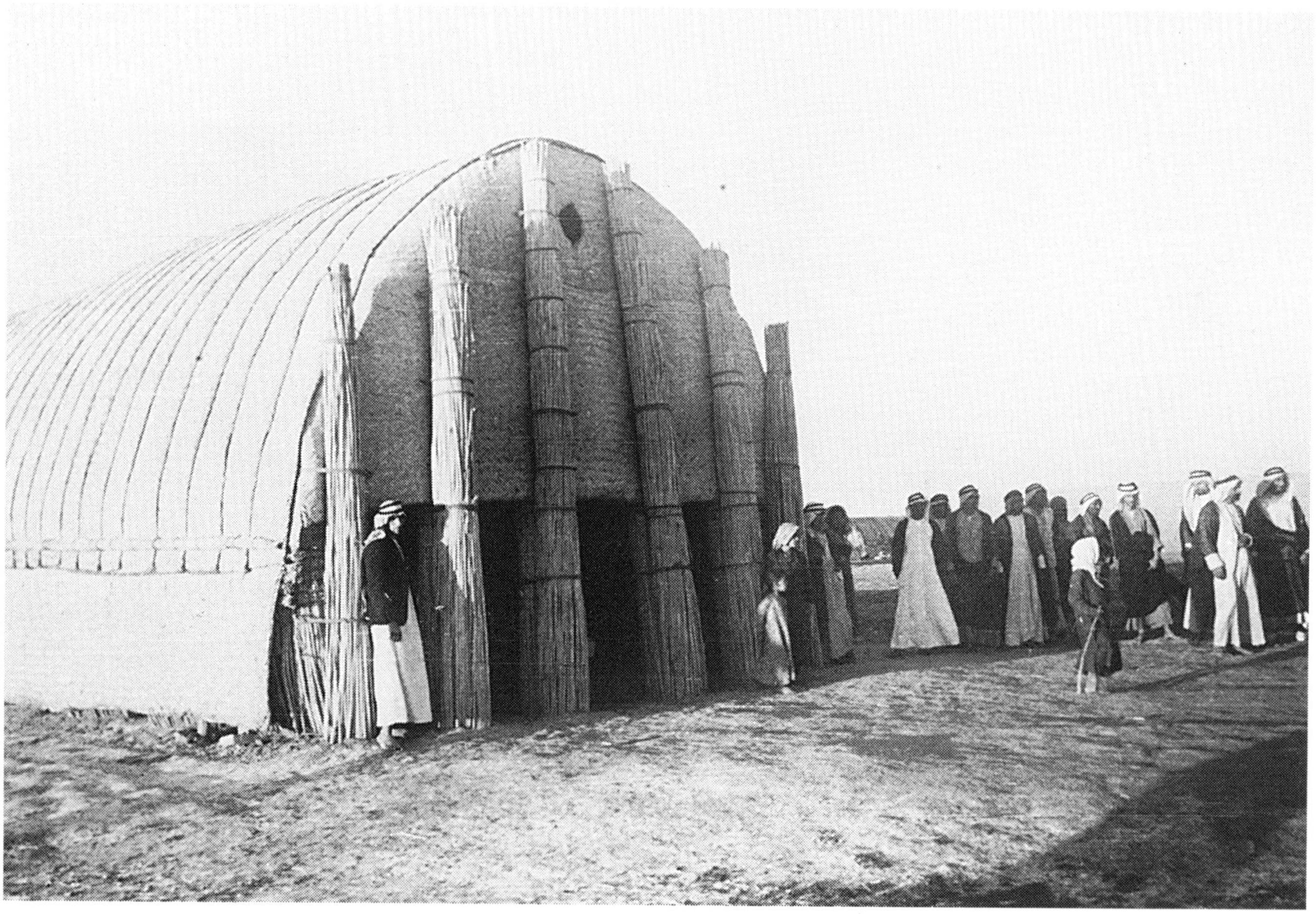

Marsh Arab *madhaf* (guest house) 1941

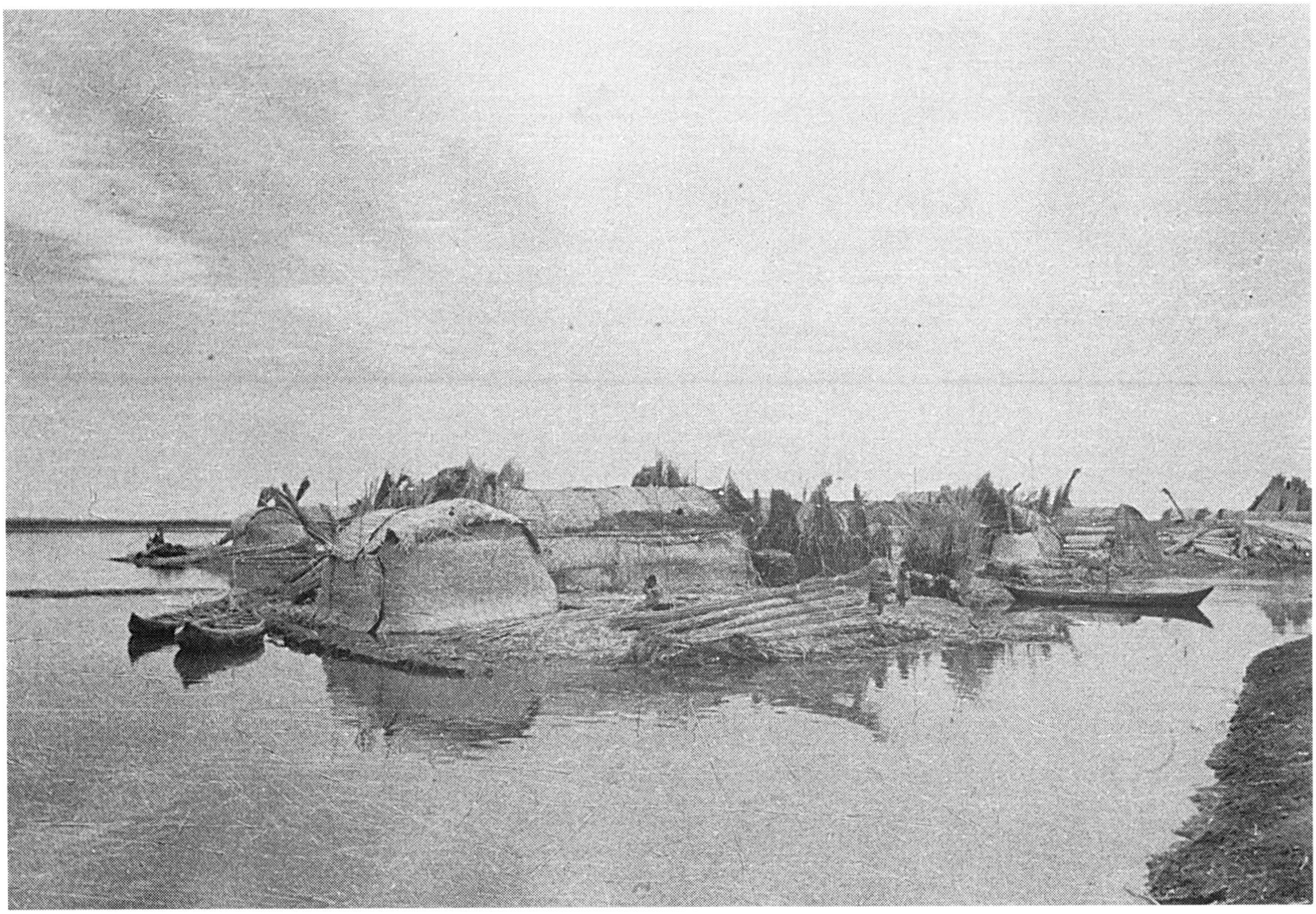

Marshes north of Basra 1941

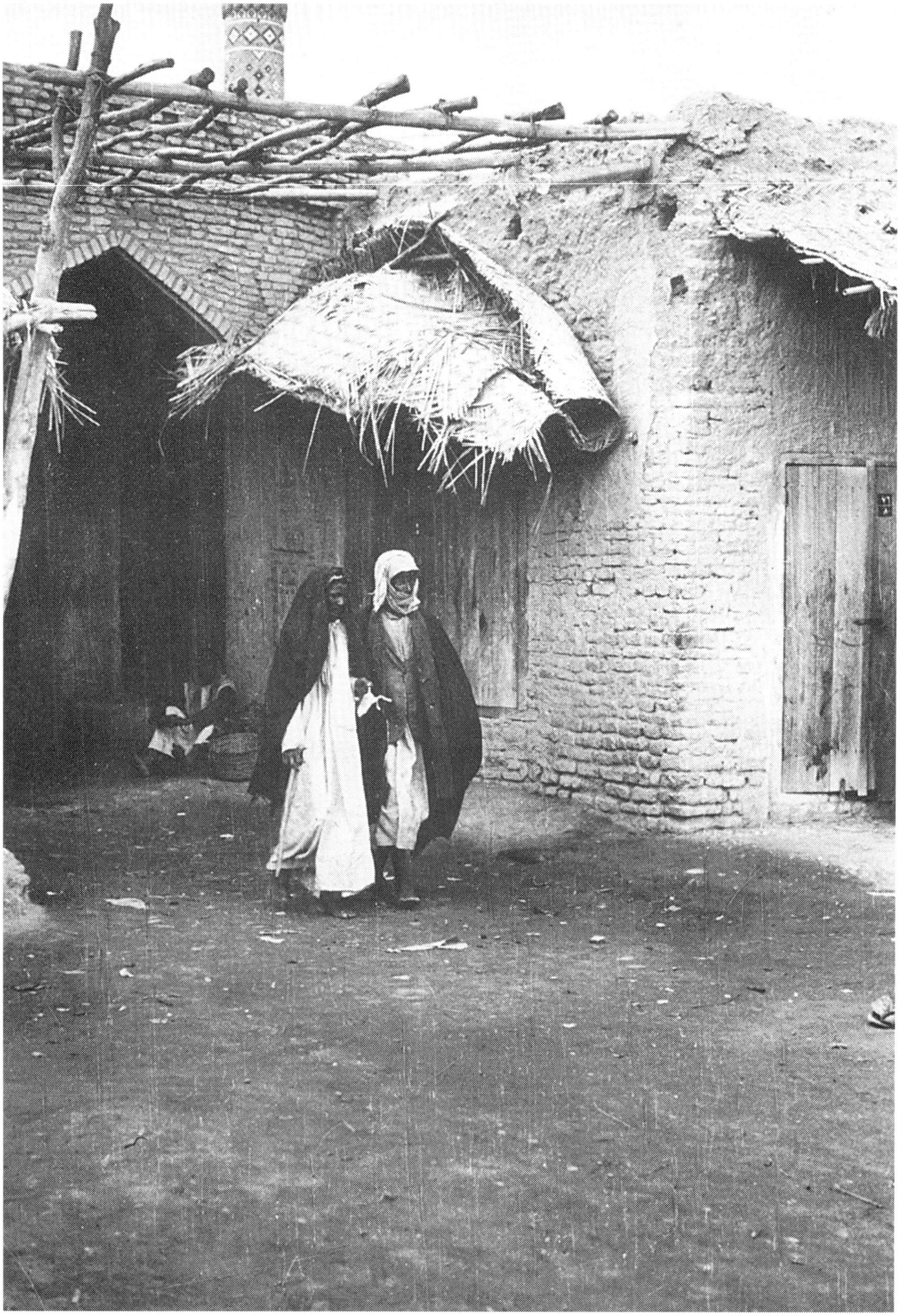

Al Zubair 1937, "all doors but no windows on the streets, for defence."

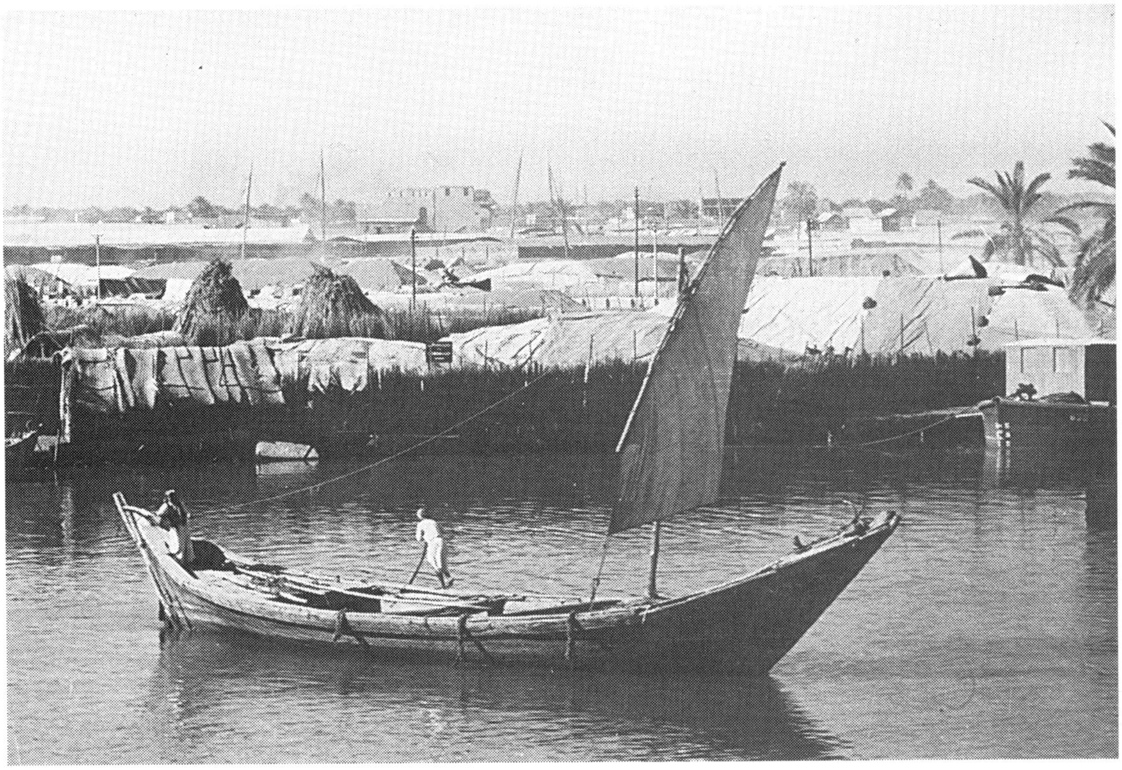

The Shatt al Arab at Basra 1937

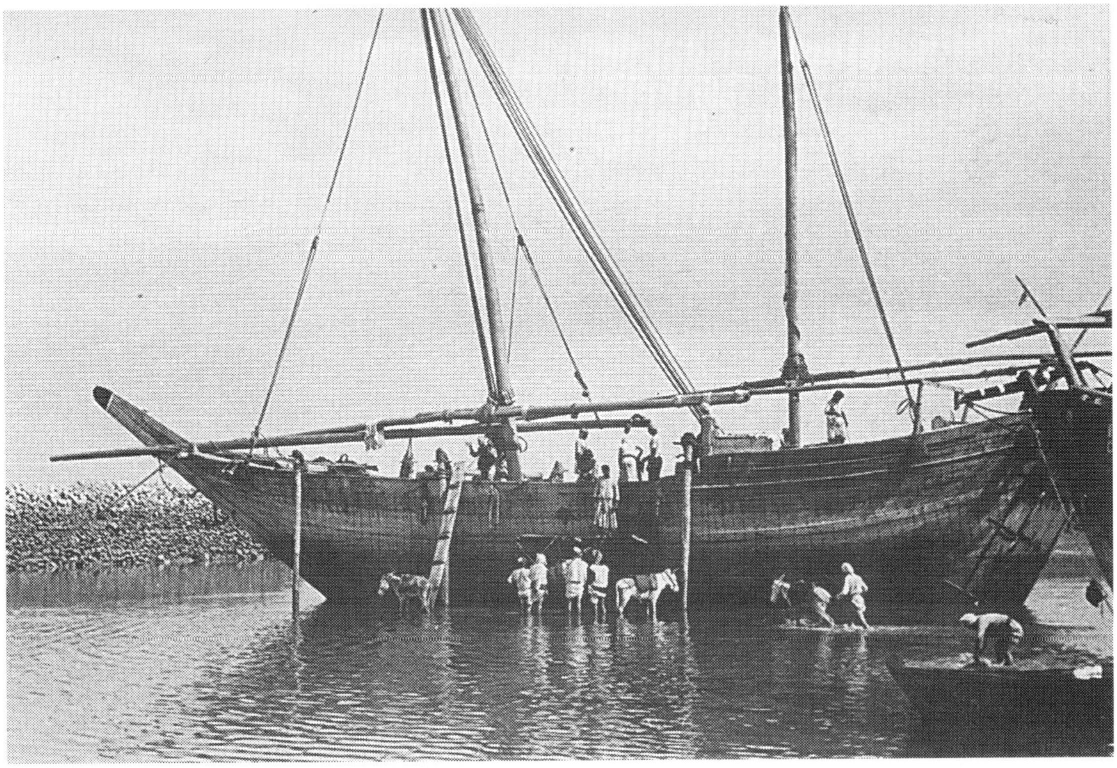

Loading water from the Shatt al Arab 1937

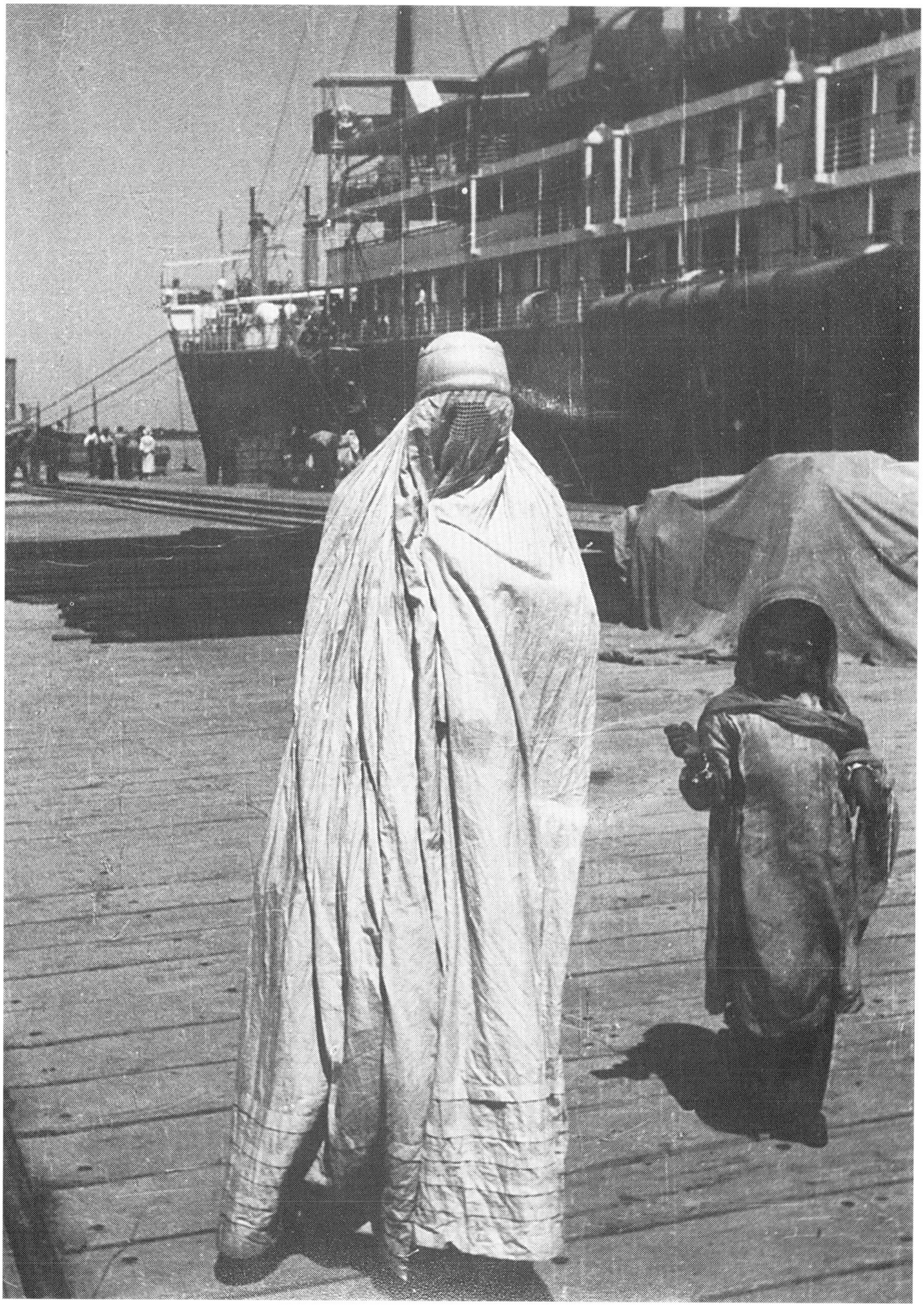

Baluchi pilgrim at Basra 1937

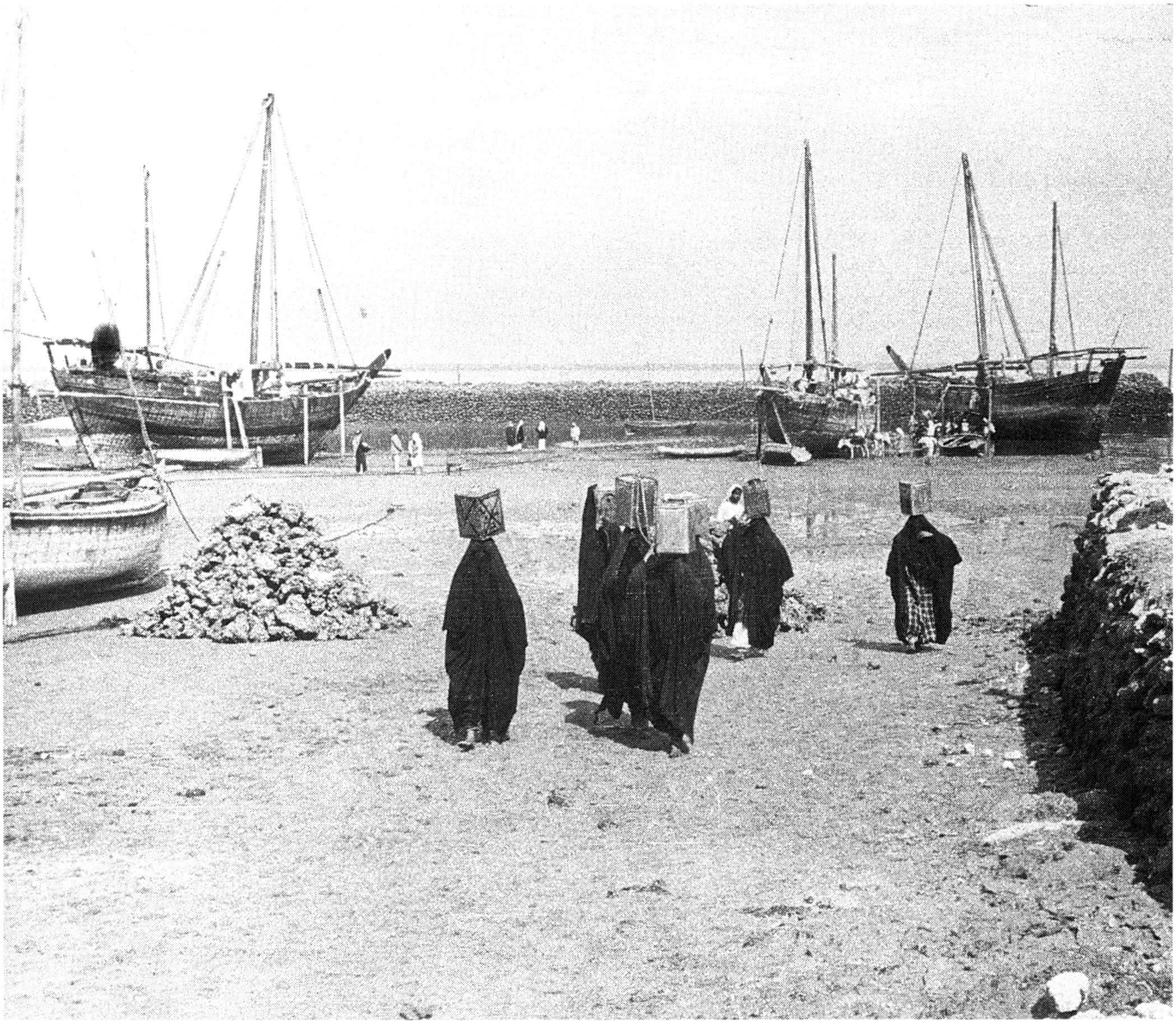

Loading fresh water on the Shatt al Arab 1937

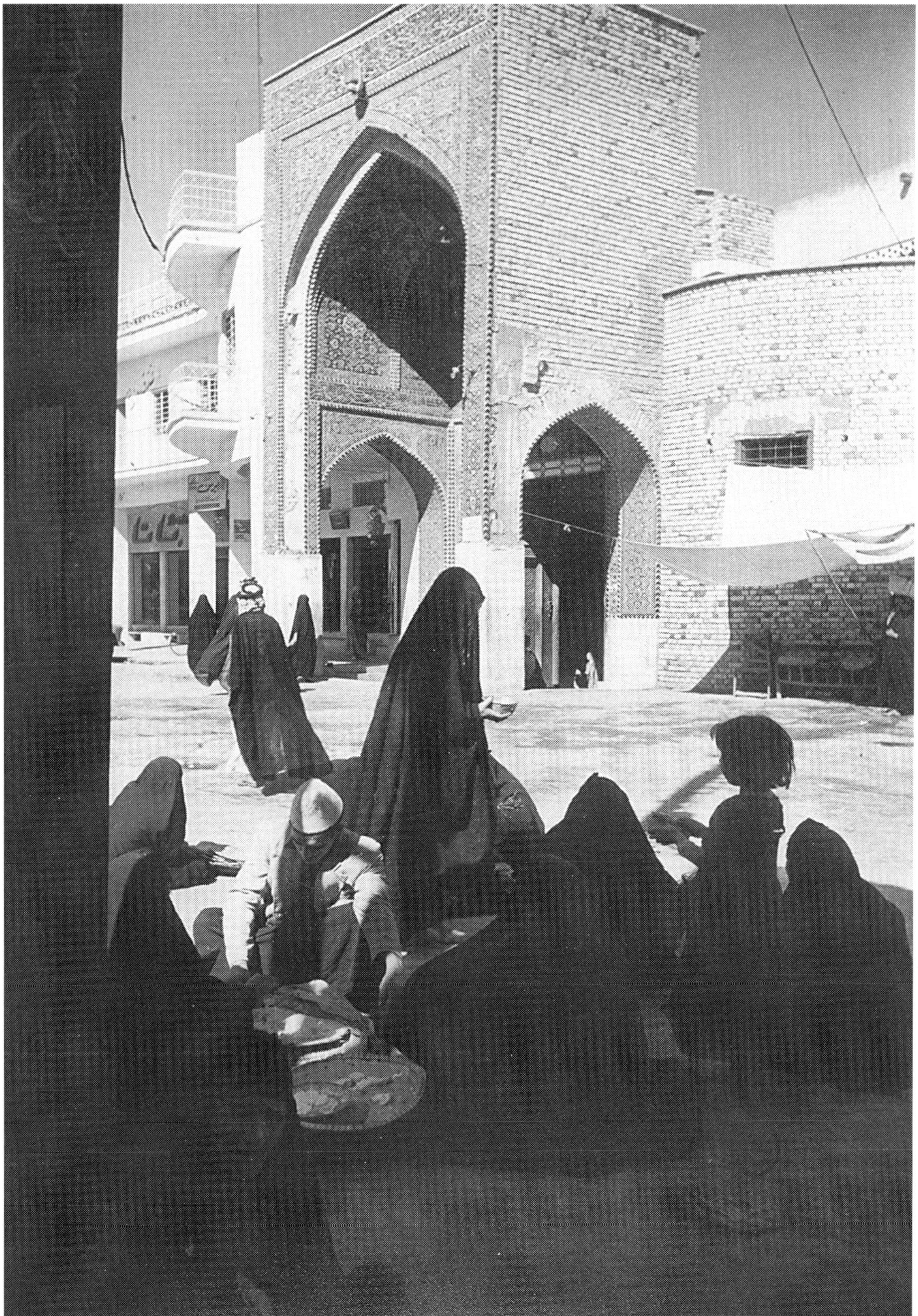

Kerbala: Shrine of the Imam Hussein 1957

KUWAIT

KUWAIT

Kuwait, the British-protected Sheikhdom lying at the head of the Gulf, was a modestly prosperous port when Freya first visited it in 1932. Oil would not be discovered until 1938, though its existence was considered likely, given the quantities already found in the Saudi province of al-Hasa further down the coast. In marked contrast to her arrival in Baghdad three years earlier, she flew there with Major (later Sir) Hubert Young, Counsellor to the High Commission in Baghdad, and his wife – an indication of the extent to which she was now considered respectable. After landing at Al Shuaiba they drove to the luxury of the Consulate and a "civilized dinner party". Next morning she visited the camp of Colonel and Mrs Dickson – he was the British Agent – who took her to Kuwait City, a small desert town of about 70,000 inhabitants "still so unwesternized that gramophones have only just been permitted and the Agent's whiskey is imported as 'lemonade'." Freya visited the market where she bought four of the Arab women's dresses that would become famous as tea-gowns. The pearl industry, affected by the world recession and by the appearance of cheap Japanese cultured pearls, was already in decline. "If one had lots of money," she told her mother, "now is the time to buy".

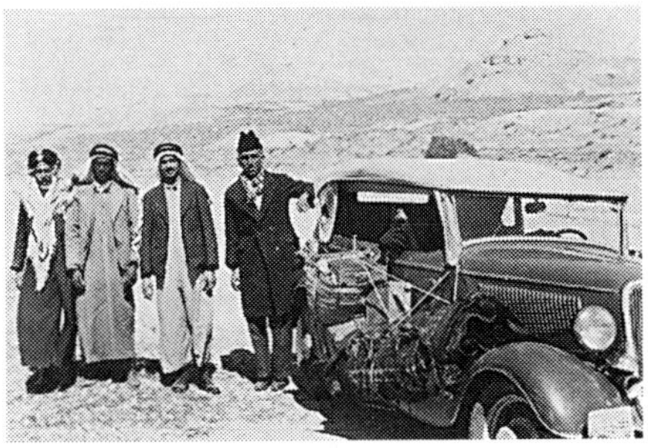

Freya's car at Zubair on way to Kuwait 1937

She enjoyed pottering round the bazaar – "a charming place, washed with the desert sun and air" with a wall and towers enclosing it, and plenty of open spaces where the Bedouin could camp in times of trouble. After the relatively cosmopolitan atmosphere of Baghdad, Freya was struck by Kuwait's puritanism. Women were not allowed outside the city walls without a written pass. The streets were solitary and windowless. The figures that moved around were mostly in white (male) or black (female), with the occasional black African face. Though slaves were no longer imported, slavery still flourished through natural increase among the slave families who supplied half the pearl divers.

Of all the sights in Kuwait Freya was most impressed by the Arab dhows in the harbour, built of shiny yellow wood from Malabar, their ribs often made out of the single forked branches of trees. "Who can describe the beauty of those boats with their high carved sterns? Or the feeling of Time turned backward as one walks along what might be the Crusading fleet drawn up for overhauling on the sands of Acre or Athlit?" She inspected the long slender *batil*, the Admiral's boat that commanded the pearling fleet; the larger *bum* that sailed as far as Zanzibar. She admired the bold and simple lines of the *sambuq*; the straight-down keel of the *jalbut* (or Jollyboat), the *bagala*, the *tarida* and the humble *huwairiyah* – most ancient craft of all, a mere bundle of reeds crafted into the shape of a boat and tied together, with a "hollow place in the middle for the fisherman to sit in the oozing water".

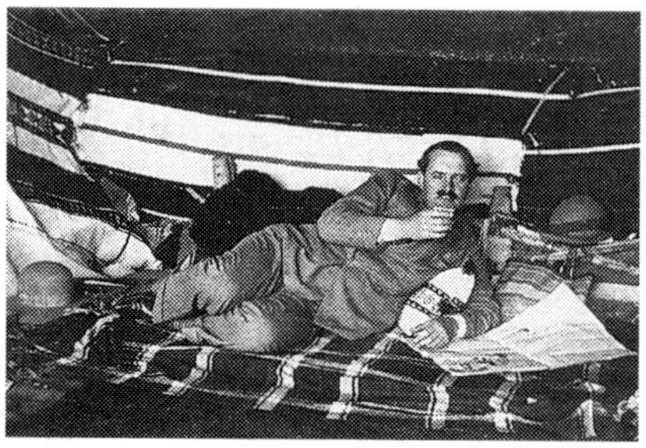

Sir Hubert Young
Head of Chancery
in Iraq 1932

On her second visit to Kuwait five years later, Freya was taken by the British Resident, Gerald de Gaury, to the island of Faylakah, a two-hour crossing by launch. They were acccompanied by Yusuf al-Mutawwa, a gentle old man who lived "on a respectable income made years ago by the selling of slaves from Mecca, to which he now – out of regard for modern convention – refers to as a trade in dates". She noted that new slaves were no longer being brought into the sheikhdom, and increasing numbers of those already there were being set free. Times were changing – though not too fast. "Civilization", she concluded, "will come tempered, more like a Marriage and less like a Rape; and the poor little town – that looks to her untried bridegroom hopefully for all temporal blessings – may yet, with gentle treatment, keep her peculiar charm."

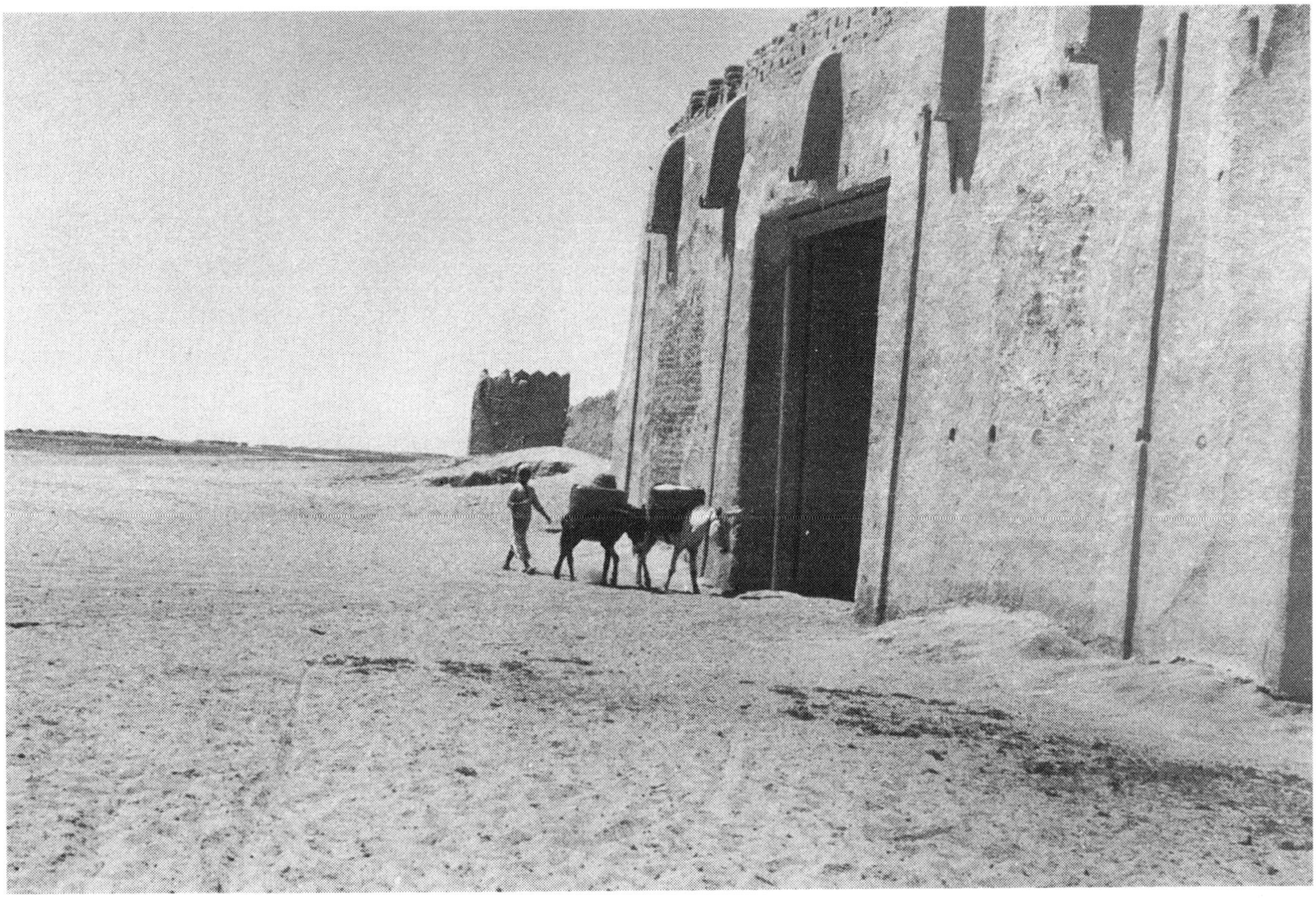

Kuwait City Walls 1937

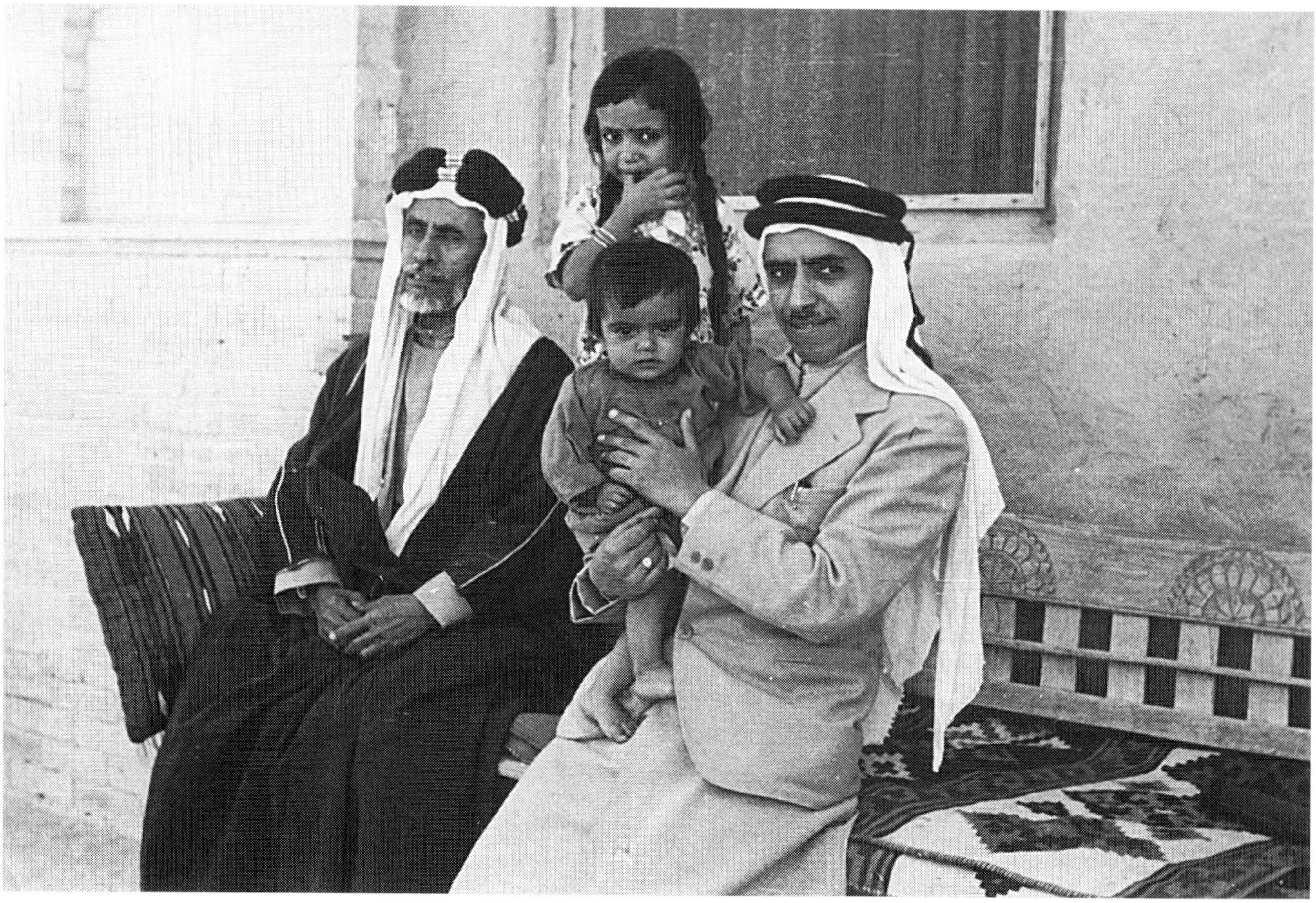

"Kuwait Citizens" 1937

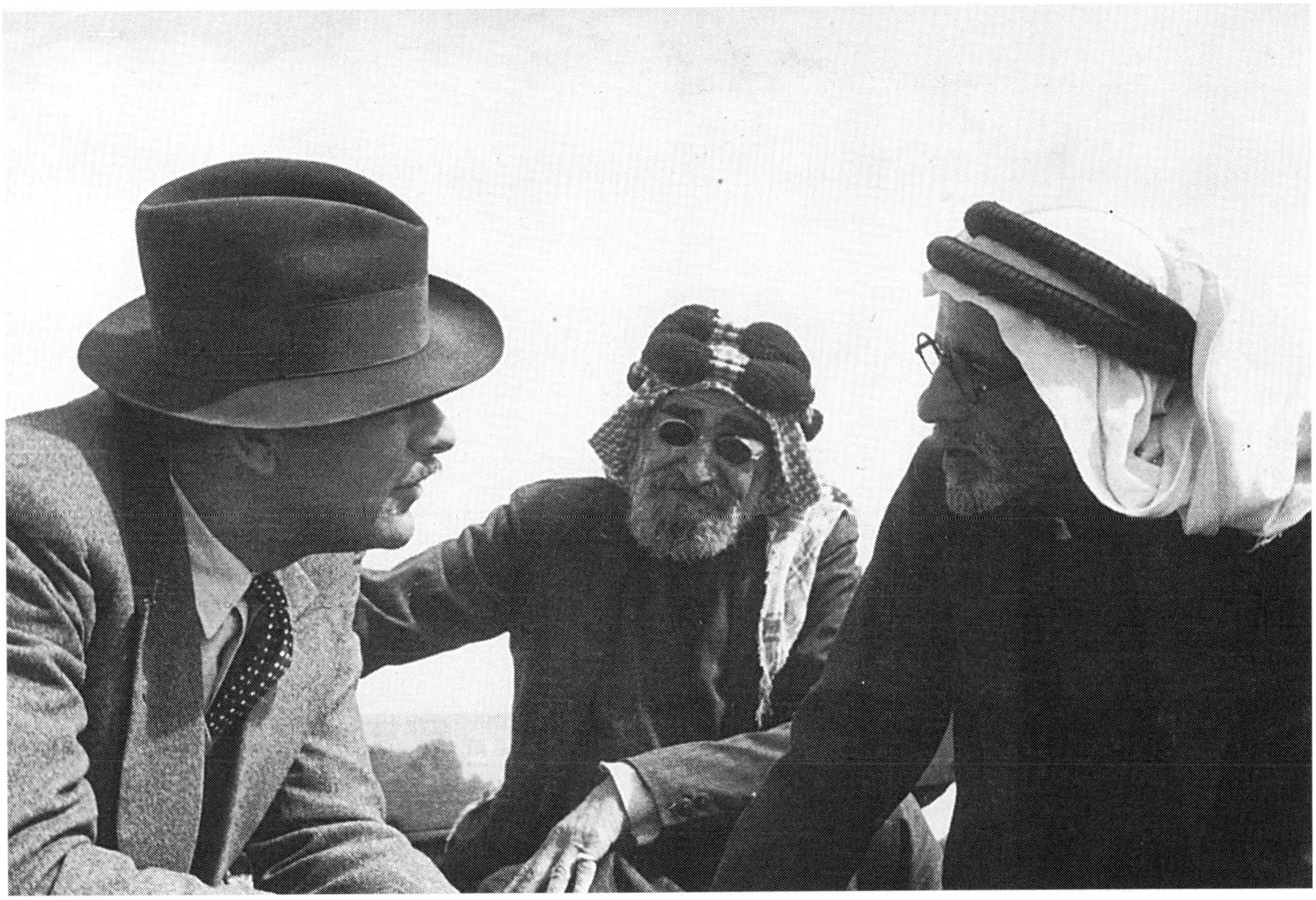

Gerald de Gaury with Yusuf al Mutawwa and friend, Faylakah Island 1937

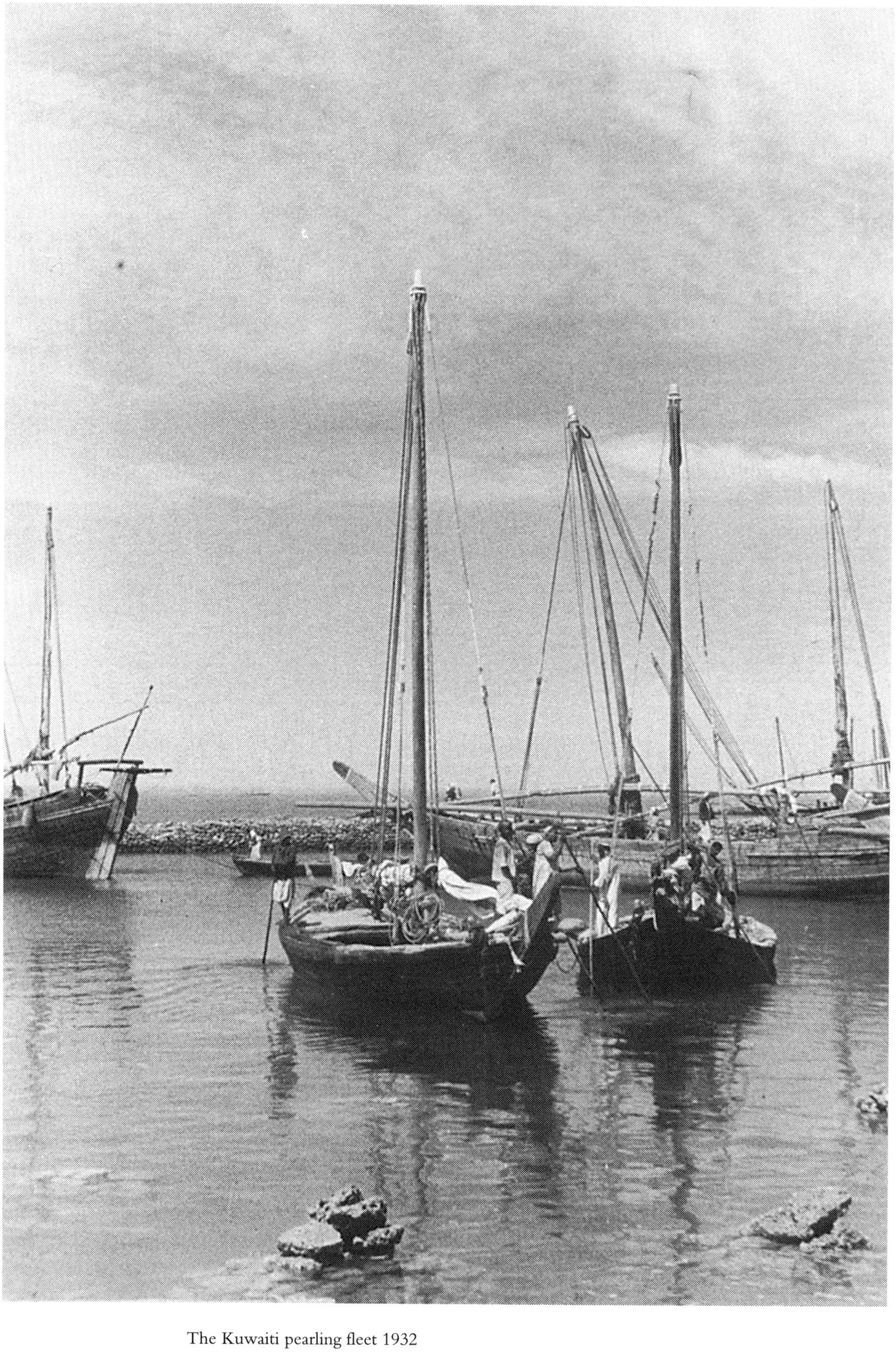

The Kuwaiti pearling fleet 1932

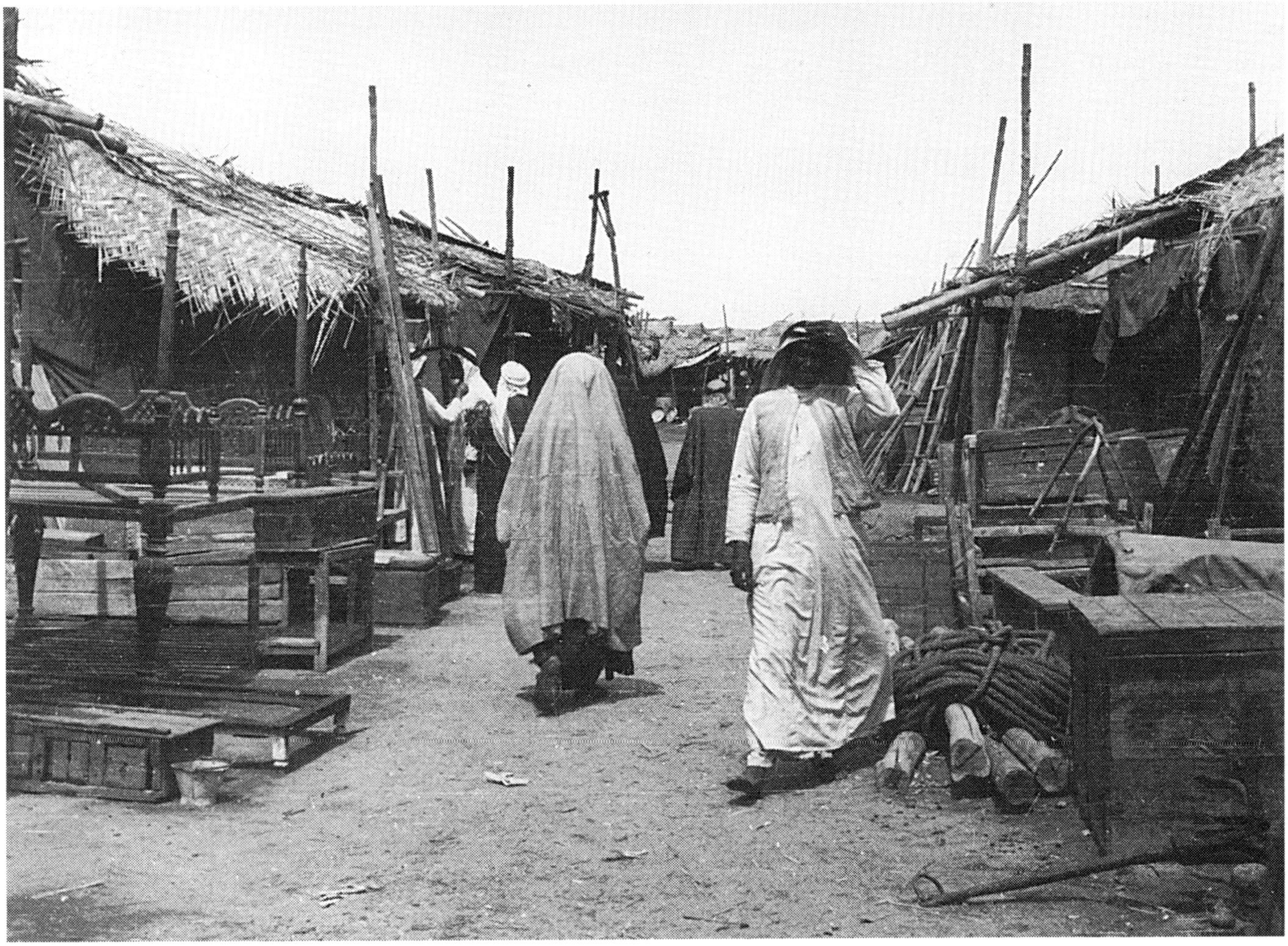

Kuwait shopping street 1937

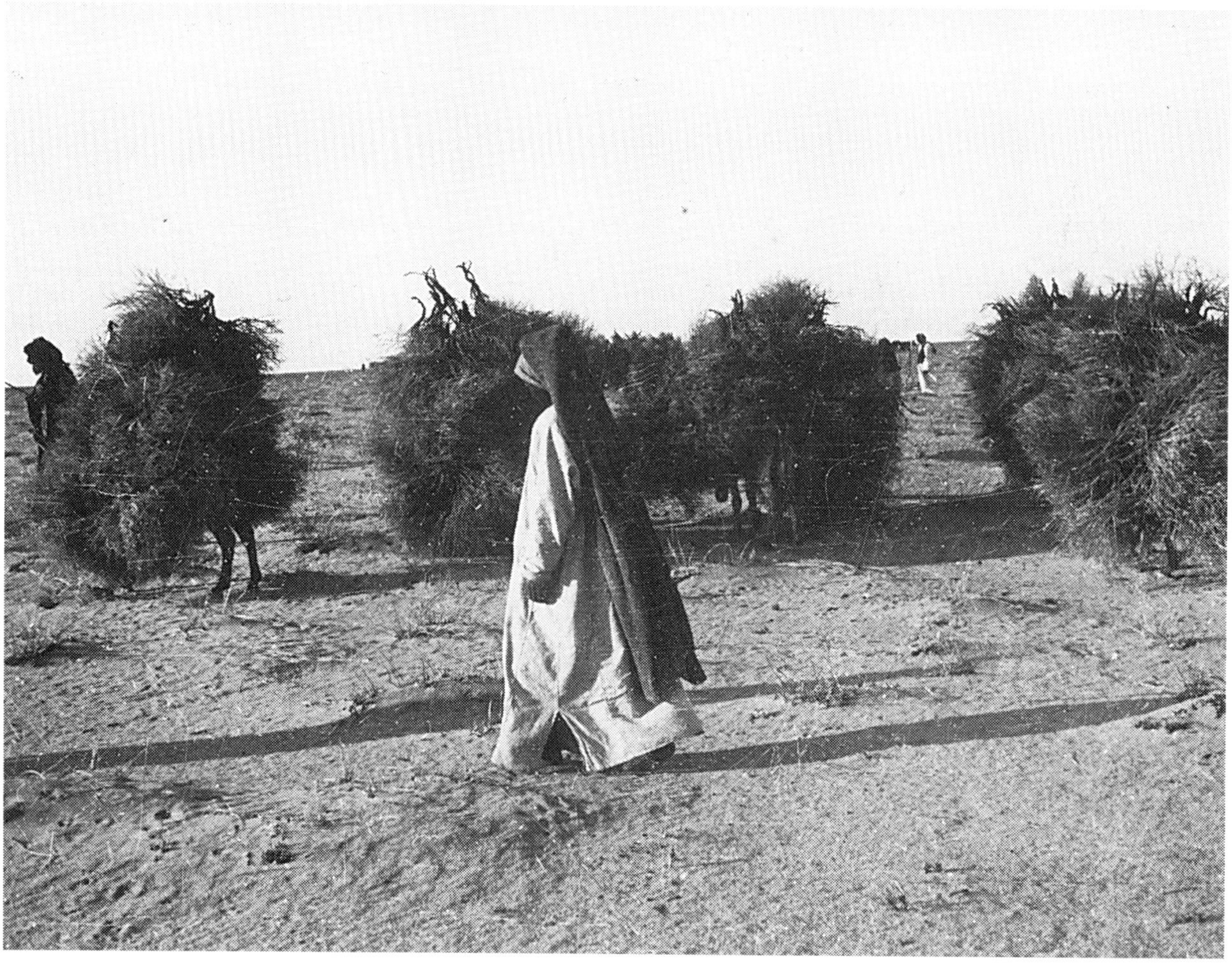

Thorn gatherers of the Mutair, Kuwait 1937

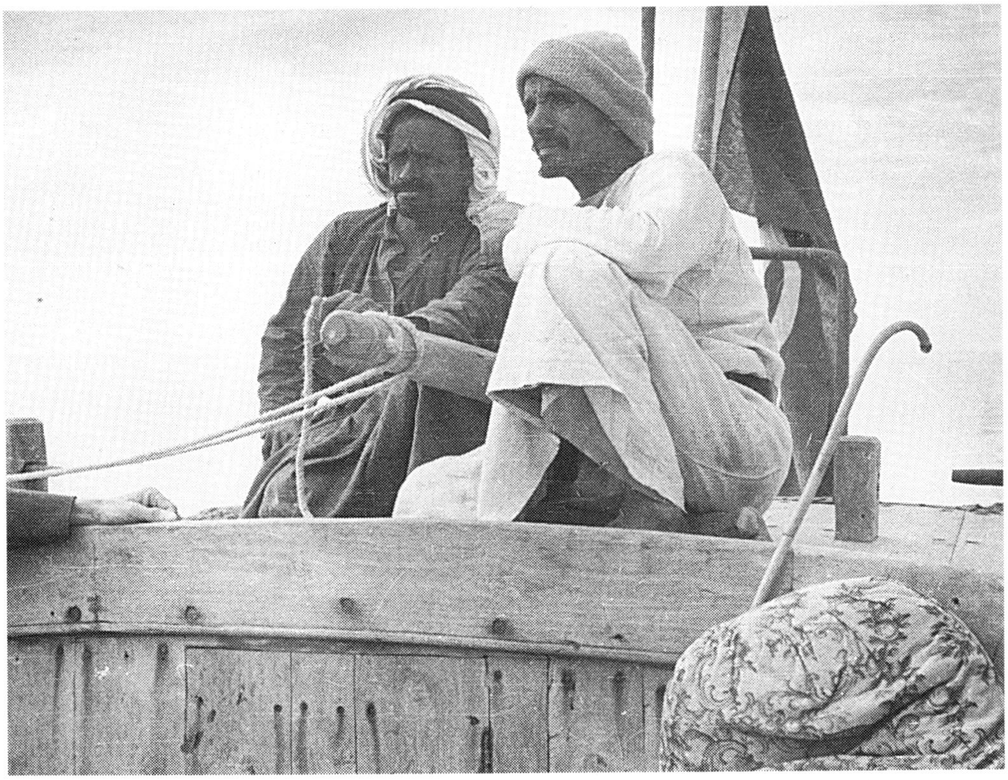

Kuwaiti helmsmen 1937

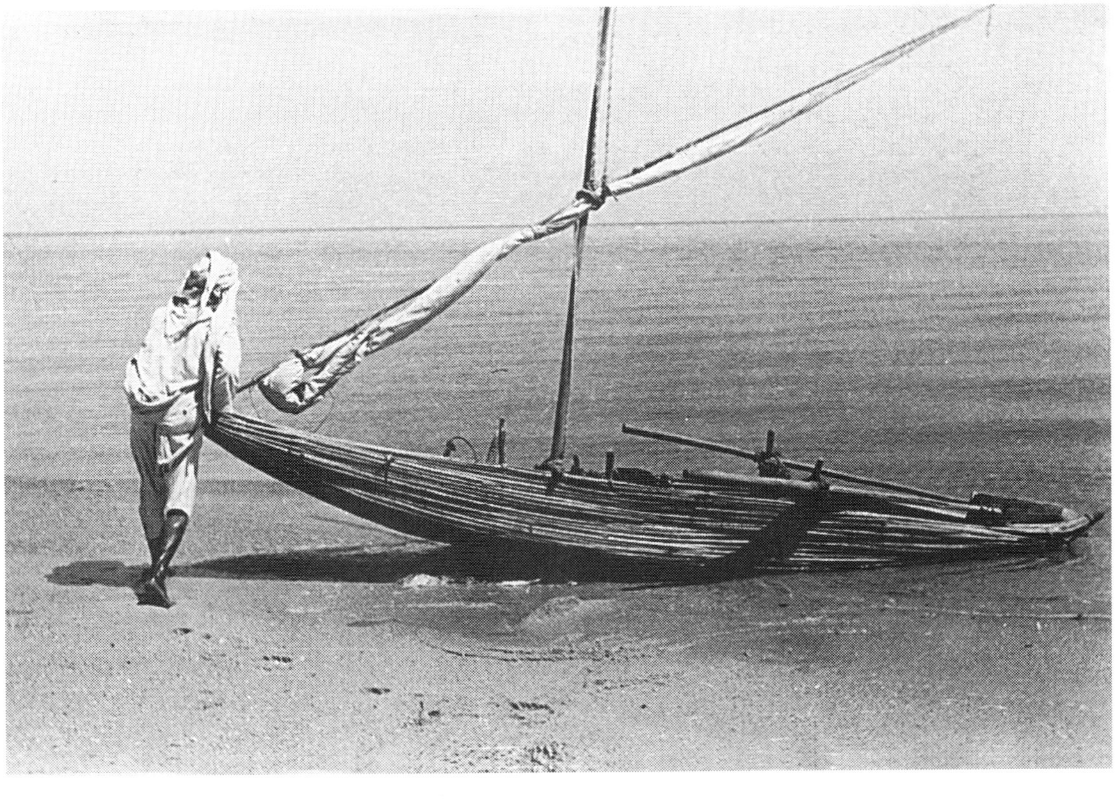

Huwairah, Kuwaiti 1937.
"The oldest craft. The water oozes through the reeds but does not sink them."

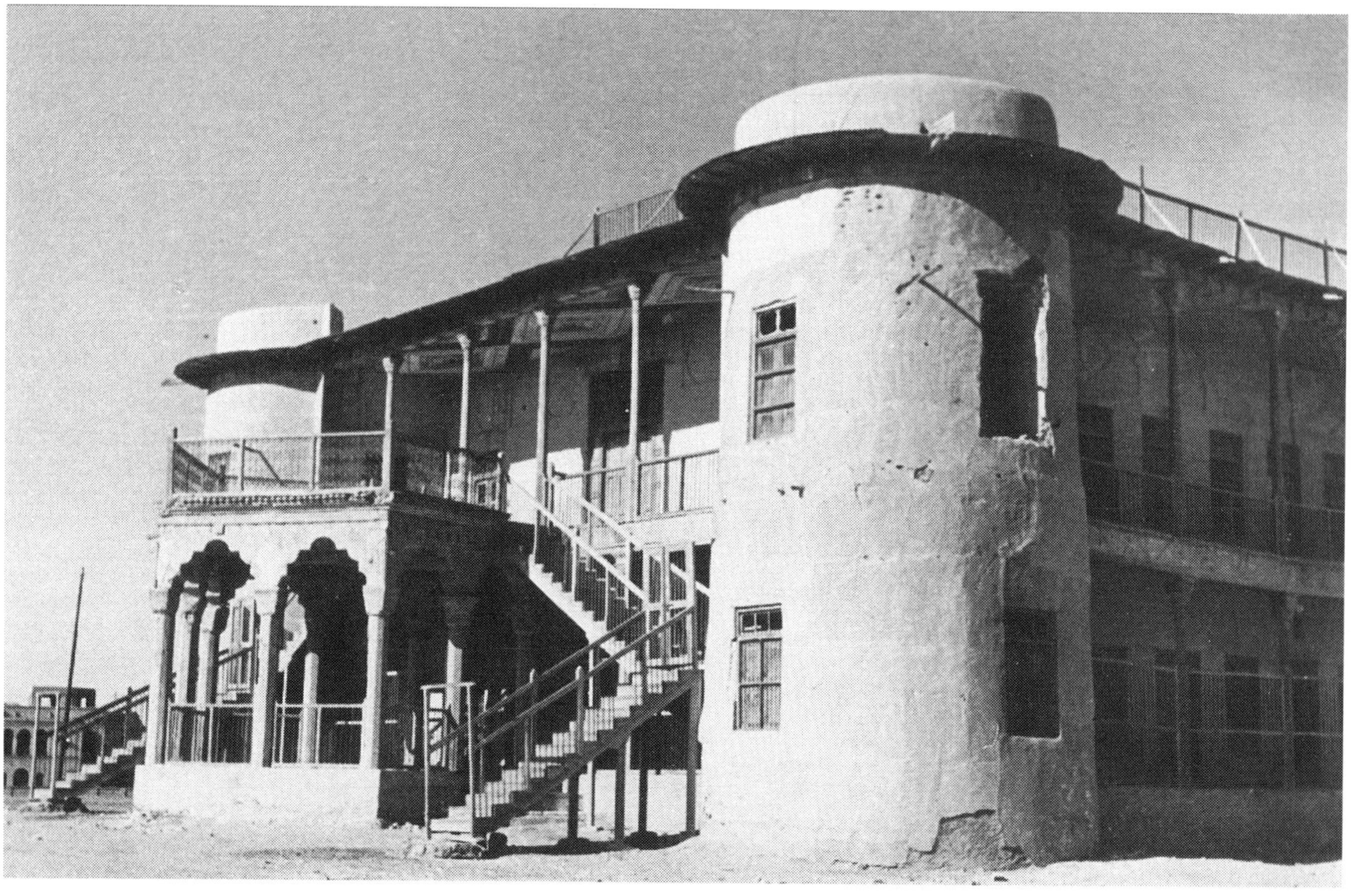

Amir's Palace 1937

CHRONOLOGY

1893	Born January 31st in Paris to Robert and Flora Stark.
1894	Sister Vera born.
1906	Loses part of her scalp in accident in Italian carpet factory.
1911	Enters Bedford College, London, boarding with Viva Jeyes. Meets Professor W. P. Ker who becomes her mentor. Robert Stark leaves his family and emigrates to Canada. Flora Stark remains in Italy.
1914	On the outbreak of war works briefly in the censorship department before volunteering as a nurse in G. M. Trevelyan's Italian ambulance unit.
1915	Serves in hospitals near Italian-Austrian front. Witnesses famous Italian retreat from Caporetto.
1921	Begins learning Arabic from her home at La Mortela near Genoa.
1923	Death of W. P. Ker while climbing with F.S. on Monte Rosa.
1926	Herbert Young, a friend of her father's, makes her his heir to the Casa Freia at Asolo, the Venetian hill town which becomes her home. Vera dies of septicaemia, following a miscarriage, leaving four young children.
1927	Enrols at the School of Oriental and African Studies in London to continue Arabic classes.
1927	December-March 1928. Spends winter in Broumana, near Beirut, improving Arabic.
1928	Visits Damascus. Expedition to Jebel Druze with Venetia Buddicom. Returns to Italy via Transjordan, Palestine and Egypt.
1929	Arrives in Baghdad.
1930–1	Visits Castles of the Assassins, and travels through Western Persia.
1932	*Baghdad Sketches* published by *Baghdad Times*.
1933	Travels in Persia earn the Royal Geographical Society's Back Memorial Grant.
1934	*Valleys of the Assassins* published to critical acclaim.
1935	First journey to the Hadhramaut in South Arabia (now Yemen).
1936	*The Southern Gates of Arabia* published.
1938	Wakefield Expedition to Hadhramaut with archaeologist Gertrude Caton Thompson.
1939	April-May: visits Crusader Castles in Syria. September: sent to Aden as assistant to Stewart Perowne in Government Information Department.
1940	February: travels to Sana'a, the Yemeni capital, to counter pro-Axis influence. June: Italy enters war - Sana'a remains neutral. September: transferred to Cairo. October: *Winter in Arabia* published. December: begins work recruiting Egyptians for anti-Axis "Brotherhood of Freedom".
1941	Divides time between Cairo and Baghdad, where she establishes Iraqi branch of the Brotherhood. May: endures siege of British Embassy by nationalist government of Rashid Ali al Gailani. Remains mostly in Baghdad till July 1942.
1942	April: visits Northern Iraq and Iraqi Kurdistan. July-October: on leave in Cyprus. Encouraged by Sir Sidney Cockerell begins work on first volume of autobiography *Traveller's Prelude*. November: Flora Stark dies in the USA. *Letter from Syria*, based on 1927-8 travels in Levant, published. Receives Founder's Gold Medal from Royal Geographic Society for travels in South Arabia.
1943	February-March: Visits Wavells in India. Drives back through Persia, selling government car at considerable profit in Tehran. October-June 1944: tours USA to defend British policy of restricting Jewish immigration into Palestine.
1944	August-January 1945: stays in England, writing *East is West*.

1945	February: flies to India to work with Lady Wavell in mustering support for Empire among Indian women. May 3rd VE Day. July: returns to Casa Freia in Asolo. Works for Ministry of Information setting up reading centres in Italy under auspices of Allied Military Government.
1947	October: marries Stewart Perowne.
1948	February: joins Perowne in Barbados, where he was Deputy Governor. July: returns to Italy and remains in Europe apart from visit to West Indies in December-March 1949. *Perseus in the Wind,* essays, published.
1950	March: joins Perowne in Libya where he has been appointed Adviser to new government of King Idris. *Traveller's Prelude* published. Visits Greece.
1951	March: returns to Asolo, deciding marriage is over. Honorary Degree from Glasgow University. *Beyond Euphrates* (autobiography vol. II), published.
1952	Marriage dissolved. Autumn: travels in Greece and Turkey.
1953	June: awarded CBE in Coronation Honours. *Coast of Incense* (autobiography vol. III) published.
1954	March-August: travels in Syria, Turkey and Greece. *Ionia: A Quest* published.
1956	May-July: visits "lost" Byzantine cities in Northern Syria and Southern Turkey. *The Lycian Shore* published.
1957	Autumn: visits Turkey, Mosul and Baghdad.
1958	July-August: visits Northern and Central Turkey. *Alexander's Path* published.
1959	Visits Iran, Greece, Lebanon and Kenya. *Riding to the Tigris* published.
1960	Visits Tunisia, Greece and Turkey
1961	Visits Cambodia, China, India, Turkey, Lebanon and Egypt. *Dust in the Lion's Paw* (autobiography vol. IV) published.
1962	Visits central Turkey.
1963	Visits Istanbul. *The Journey's Echo* - an anthology, published.
1964	Begins building Montoria, new house outside Asolo.
1966	Sells Casa Freia to Asolo municipality. Visits Greece and Turkey. *Rome on the Euphrates* published.
1967	September: visits Afghanistan, Samarkand, Bukhara and Tashkent.
1968	Visits Afghanistan and Greece. *The Zodiac Arch*, anthology, published.
1970	November: visits Nepal. *The Minaret of Djam* published.
1972	Becomes Dame of the British Empire in New Year's Honours.
1973	Sells Montoria, moves to flat in Asolo. Visits Kashmir.
1975	Visits Bodrum and Istanbul in Turkey.
1976	March: visits Sana'a, North Yemen and Southern Turkey. Stays with Queen Mother in Castle of Mey. *A Peak in Darien*, essays, published.
1977	To Syria with BBC television crew for journey down the Euphrates on specially constructed raft.
1984	Revisits Nepal with BBC television crew.
1985	Receives Freedom of the City of Asolo.
1993	31 January: celebrates 100th birthday.
1993	9 May: dies at her home in Asolo.

All of Freya Stark's books are published by John Murray with the exception of eight volumes of letters edited by Lucy and Caroline Moorehead, published by Michael Russell between 1974 and 1982. A book of photographs of South Arabia, *Seen in the Hadhramaut*, appeared in 1938. *Over the Rim of the World*, a selection of letters edited by Caroline Moorehead, published by Murrays in association with Michael Russell, appeared in 1988. Books about Freya Stark include *A Tower in the Wall* by Alexander Maitland (Blackwood 1982), *Traveller Through Time* by Malise Ruthven (Viking 1986), *Freya Stark* by Caroline Moorehead (Penguin 1986) and *Freya Stark – a biography* by Molly Izzard (Hodder & Stoughton 1993).